Warman's®
Modern
U.S. Coins
FIELD GUIDE

☟ W9-AVH-581

Arlyn G. Sieber

Published by

Krause Publications, a division of F+W Media, Inc.
700 East State Street • Iola, WI 54990-0001
715-445-2214 • 888-457-2873
www.krausebooks.com

To order books or other products call toll-free 1-800-258-0929
or visit us online at www.krausebooks.com or www.Shop.Collect.com

Library of Congress Control Number: 2010923993

ISBN-13: 978-1-4402-1380-9

ISBN-10: 1-4402-1380-1

Designed by Katrina Newby
Edited by Justin Moen

Printed in China

ACKNOWLEDGMENTS

The author gratefully acknowledges the following for their assistance in producing this book:

Joel Edler
Kris Kandler
Paul Kennedy
Clifford Mishler
Justin Moen
Ken Potter
Heritage Numismatic Auctions, Inc.
    3500 Maple Ave., 17th Floor
    Dallas, TX 75219-3941
    214-528-3500
    800-US COINS (872-6467)
    http://coins.ha.com
U.S. Mint (www.usmint.gov)

CONTENTS

Introduction 7

Welcome to Coin Collecting. 14

The Coin Community 26

How to Collect Modern U.S. Coins. 42

How to Handle and Store Coins 49

State of the Market. 61

About the Value Listings 64

Lincoln Bicentennial Cents (2009). 68

Westward Journey Nickels (2004-2005) 75

50 State Quarters (1999-2008) 81

D.C. and U.S. Territories Quarters (2009) 134

America the Beautiful Quarters (2010-2021). 142

Presidential Dollars (2007-2016) 152

Native American Dollars (2009-) 172

First Spouse Gold $10 (2007-2016) 177

Ultrahigh-Relief Gold $20 (2009) 196

Commemoratives (1982-) 200

Commemorative Sets (1983-) 306

Uncirculated Sets (1984-) 325

Proof Sets (1982-) 328

Silver American Eagle Bullion Coins (1986-) 405

Silver America the Beautiful Bullion Coins (2010-2021) 425

Gold American Eagle Bullion Coins (1986-) 433

Gold American Buffalo Bullion Coins (2006-) 466

Platinum American Eagle Bullion Coins (1997-) 476

Glossary 508

2008 50 State Quarters Silver Proof Set

Modern U.S. coins have attracted millions of collectors worldwide.

INTRODUCTION

"Modern" is a relative term. Sometimes we think of any object from our individual lifetime as modern, but succeeding generations may not. Some antiques purists consider any item less than 100 years old to be modern. Some numismatic scholars consider any coin mass-produced by machinery to be modern.

Sometimes an important development provides the demarcation for modern. In 1955, for example, Chevrolet introduced a new V-8 engine. The automaker had not produced a V-8 since 1918, and this new, "modern" version in 1955 provided the basis for Chevrolet V-8 engines for years to come.

In 1982, the U.S. Mint issued a half dollar commemorating the 250th anniversary of George Washington's birth. The coin was struck in the traditional 90-percent-silver composition and was offered in uncirculated and proof versions. It was a huge success; the Mint sold more than 2.2 million uncirculated versions and almost 4.9 million proof versions.

The Washington half dollar was the first U.S. commemorative coin in 28 years. The first U.S. commemorative was an 1892 half dollar for the Columbian Exposition, which was held in 1893 in Chicago to commemorate the 400th anniversary of

The first U.S. commemorative, the 1892 Columbian Exposition half dollar, commemorated the 400th anniversary of Columbus' voyage to the New World. The Columbian half dollar opened the door to many other commemorative coins from the 1910s-1950s.

Columbus' voyage to the New World. The Columbian half dollar opened the door to many other commemorative coins from the 1910s and continuing into the 1950s. Most were silver half dollars, but there was also an 1893 quarter (also for the Columbian Exposition), a number of gold dollars, two gold $2.50 coins, and two gold $50 coins.

The 1930s saw a proliferation of U.S. commemorative coins. They were sold by the Mint at premiums above face value with a portion of the proceeds benefiting some organization or event related to the coin's theme. Some of the coins commemorated state anniversaries or national themes, such as the U.S. Sesquicentennial in 1926 and the 75th anniversary of the Battle of Gettysburg in 1936.

Others, however, were of little national importance, such as issues for the Cincinnati Music Center and the centennial of Elgin, Ill., in 1936. Commemorative coins had become an easy mark for members of Congress looking to raise funds for a pet project.

Congress grew weary of U.S. coinage being used as local fundraisers, and the flow of commemorative coins slowed in the 1940s and '50s. The last commemorative before the 28-year hiatus was a 1954 half dollar honoring Booker T. Washington and George Washington Carver.

The 1982 Washington half dollar opened the door to many other commemorative issues. Except for 1985, the United States has issued commemorative coins every year since 1982.

The commemoratives issued from 1892-1954 became commonly known as "early commemoratives" in the coin-collecting hobby. The issues since 1982 became commonly known as "modern commemoratives."

The "modern commemoratives," in turn, opened the door to circulating issues with commemorative and collectible aspects. Prominent among them are the 50 State Quarters, issued from

In 1982, the U.S. Mint issued a half dollar commemorating the 250th anniversary of George Washington's birth. It was the first U.S. commemorative coin released in 28 years, and it was a huge success; the Mint sold more than 2.2 million uncirculated versions and almost 4.9 million proof versions. Except for 1985, the U.S. has issued commemorative coins every year since 1982.

1999-2008. Also among them are the Westward Journey Nickels (2004-2006) and the Lincoln Bicentennial Cents (2009). The America the Beautiful Quarters series, which commemorates the nation's national parks and sites, began in 2010 and is scheduled to run through 2021.

Thus, this book covers "modern" U.S. coins—those issued since 1982. The focus is on coins with intentional collectible aspects to them—such as the aforementioned Lincoln

Modern commemoratives opened the door to circulating issues with commemorative and collectible aspects. Prominent among them were the 50 State Quarters, issued from 1999-2008. The U.S. Mint once estimated that 147 million people collected the 50 State Quarters.

cents, Westward nickels, and State quarters—rather than the typical circulation issues or unintentional varieties ("error coins") of circulation issues.

The proliferation of these collectible coins issued since 1982 has spawned a new genre of coin collecting. Previously, collecting U.S. coins consisted of buying coins from the late 1700s, 1800s, or early 1900s from professional dealers at the going market rate or searching circulation coinage for the different date and mintmark combinations of a series with the same design, such as Jefferson nickels. Both continue to play important roles in today's coin hobby.

Since 1982, however, collectors can also now look for coins with different designs in their pocket change and seek to complete a series from circulation. For the cost of the coins' face value and an inexpensive folder to put them in, entire families have joined in the search and shared in the excitement of finding an issue that fills a previously empty spot in their collection. The U.S. Mint once estimated that 147 million people collected the 50 State Quarters.

Collectors can also purchase current-year commemoratives and proof coins from the U.S. Mint or search for past issues at coin shops and coin shows, or through advertisements in hobby publications such as *Coins, Coin Prices,* and *Numismatic News.*

This book is a guide to this new genre of collecting. It lists what has been issued in the past and documents why it was issued, and what is scheduled to be issued in the future. With many more offerings to come, the "modern" era of coin collecting will continue for many years to come.

2009 Proof Set

WELCOME TO COIN COLLECTING

The kingdom of Lydia, which was located in part of modern-day Turkey, is credited with producing the world's first coins in 700-650 B.C. Some speculate that the world's first coin collector came shortly thereafter.

Coin collecting has provided an enjoyable, educational, and sometimes profitable pastime for generations. The hobby welcomes those of all ages, physical abilities, and financial means. All it requires is an interest in the subject, enjoyment in pursuing a collecting goal, and satisfaction in the completion of that goal. The reward is the pride a collector feels when he or she pulls a coin album off their bookshelf and views a complete collection of a particular coin type or series, or even the progress made toward completing a collection.

Printed references to coin collecting date back as far as the 15th century. In 1796, the hobby generated the first widely circulated book on numismatics: "The Virtuoso's Companion and Coin Collector's Guide," published in England. Coinage was scarce in Colonial America, so there were few coins to collect and even fewer with the financial wherewithal to put coins aside and not spend them.

Congress passed an act establishing the U.S. Mint on April 2, 1792. The decimal coinage system it authorized was based largely

A gold stater for King Croesus of Lydia. Lydia, which was located in part of modern-day Turkey, is credited with producing the world's first coins in 700-650 B.C.

1792 half disme

on a plan put forth by Thomas Jefferson. The following July, it produced 1,500 silver "half dismes," or 5-cent pieces, which are regarded as the nation's first official coinage.

U.S. coinage began in earnest in 1793 with the production of more than 35,000 copper half cents and more than 36,000 copper one-cent coins. By 1796, in addition to half cents and cents, the Mint was producing silver half dimes, dimes, quarters, half dollars, dollars, and gold $2.50, $5, and $10 coins. By the mid-1800s, the Mint was producing about 17 million coins annually in 12 denominations.

The increased production meant more coins to collect, and there were more people who could afford to collect them. A few magazines devoted to coin collecting began to appear in the middle of the century. So did dealers who bought and sold collectible coins for a living or as a supplement to their day jobs. The magazines contained advertisements for collectible coins and oftentimes were produced as house organs and marketing tools by the dealers themselves.

Many collectors of the time also courted relationships with banks, bullion-exchange houses, or other volume handlers of coins as sources for their collections. Those who lived near Philadelphia cultivated relationships with officials and employees of the U.S. Mint's production facility located there and thus obtained coins directly from the Mint.

Interest in coin collecting in the U.S. surged in the late 1850s when the smaller, copper-nickel Flying Eagle cent replaced the old

At top is the 1793 half-cent coin. On the bottom is the 1793 one-cent coin.

The large one-cent coin (top) was replaced by the smaller one-cent coin in the late 1850s (bottom).

large copper one-cent coin. Two years later, the Indian Head cent replaced the Flying Eagle cent. The general public started putting aside the obsolete coins, and demand and prices for them rose. Professional coin dealers emerged to meet the demand, and by the 1870s, most major Eastern cities had coin clubs.

The next major development in coin collecting occurred in 1888 when Dr. George Heath of Monroe, Mich.—a physician by trade who moonlighted as a mail-order coin dealer—published the first issue of *The American Numismatist*. Like many other publications of the time, the magazine was a marketing tool for Heath's coin business. In his new magazine, the country doctor estimated the number of U.S. coin collectors at 20,000.

By 1891, Heath had shortened the serial's title to *The Numismatist*, and its readership formed the basis for the founding of the American Numismatic Association. The ANA (www.money.org) continues today as the nation's largest organization for coin collectors, and *The Numismatist* continues as its official monthly journal.

Coin collecting continued to grow in the early 20th century as exciting new designs made old coins obsolete. Ironically, the Great Depression brought another major development in coin collecting that defined the hobby for years to come and still impacts it today.

In 1934, the Whitman Publishing Co. of Racine, Wis., introduced the "penny board." It was essentially a big piece of cardboard with holes in it for each date and mintmark of Lincoln

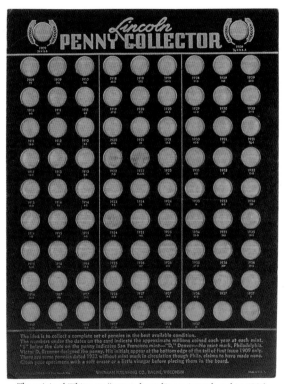

The original Whitman "penny board" was introduced in 1934.

cents, starting in 1909. The boards sold for 25 cents each and were widely available in hardware stores, dime stores, shoeshine parlors, and gasoline stations.

The boards provided cheap entertainment during the economic struggles of the 1930s as people of all ages checked the one-cent coins in their pocket change for dates and mintmarks that would fill an empty hole in the board. In 1940, the board was reconfigured into a blue folder. The blue Whitman folders and similar products from other companies continue today to provide direction in collecting a particular series and a storage and display medium for collectors.

Coin collecting enjoyed a boom period in the 1950s. War veterans and others had disposable income to devote to a hobby and could find coins of the late 1800s and early 1900s in circulation. What they couldn't find, they could buy from the growing number of dealers who operated shops, set up at coin shows, or advertised in coin publications such as the newly founded *Numismatic News*.

Today, coin collecting is enjoying another renaissance thanks in part to the various series of modern collectible U.S. coins covered in this book. Many cities and even smaller towns have coin shops. Major coin auction houses make national headlines when they sell some of numismatics' great rarities. Local, state, and regional organizations for coin collectors meet regularly and sponsor shows where collectors can browse the offerings of dozens or even hundreds of dealers in one spot. Many of these shows also

Coin shows big and small bring together collectors and dealers.

feature non-commercial displays of coins and other numismatic items set up by collectors to the benefit of their fellow hobbyists.

The ANA sponsors three shows annually in different cities across the nation. In addition to the bourse floor, the gatherings offer seminars and organization meetings that promote education and camaraderie among fellow collectors. The ANA's headquarters in Colorado Springs, Colo., features a world-class museum open to all and an extensive reference library that members can use for free.

Some lament that "valuable" coins, such as those collectors were plucking from circulation in the 1950s, can't be found in circulation anymore. But many of the coins that today's veteran hobbyists cut their collecting teeth on weren't "valuable" at the time and have never become valuable. The emphasis wasn't on value; it was on the satisfaction and enjoyment of building a collection. It was on the thrill of finding a long-sought piece needed for a collection. Many of the circulating modern series of U.S. coins revive those thrills of past coin-collecting eras.

The American Numismatic Association's headquarters in Colorado Springs, Colo., includes a world-class museum that is open to the public. Photo courtesy of ANA.

THE COIN COMMUNITY

Coin collecting can accommodate any personality type. For those who like solitude, there can be peaceful evenings searching rolls of coins, admiring a completed collection or one in progress, or opening a book or magazine on the subject. For those who like camaraderie, there is an entire community out there that shares their interest and numerous venues for bringing them together. Following is an overview of the coin community at large and resources for learning more about coins.

Coin collecting appeals to a wide range of people.

ORGANIZATIONS
National

The American Numismatic Association, founded in 1891 and federally chartered, is the nation's largest organization for coin collectors. Its headquarters in Colorado Springs, Colo., houses a first-class museum, the Edward C. Rochette Money Museum, which is open to the public.

Membership benefits include a subscription to *The Numismatist*, the association's official journal. Each monthly issue features articles on a wide range of numismatic topics along with reports on association news and events.

Members can also borrow books, auction catalogs, slide sets, and videos from the ANA's library, the Dwight N. Manley Library, which boasts more than 50,000 items. Members who borrow items pay for postage and insurance but no additional fee.

The ANA sponsors seminars on a wide range of numismatic topics at various locales throughout the country. Prominent among them is the association's Summer Seminar series, held annually in late June and early July at its headquarters in Colorado Springs. Attendance at the multi-day courses is designed to be affordable with a variety of lodging options and a meal plan.

The ANA also takes its seminar program on the road to the association's annual conventions and to events sponsored by other numismatic organizations.

The American Numismatic Association headquarters in Colorado Springs, Colo. Photo courtesy of ANA.

Regional

Regional coin organizations focus their activities on a certain part of the country, such as the Northeast or Midwest. Residency in the region, however, is usually not required for membership.

Prominent among these groups are the Central States Numismatic Society, Great Eastern Numismatic Association, New England Numismatic Association, and Pacific Northwest Numismatic Association. In addition, the Florida United Numismatists sponsors a large show and convention in January each year and boasts a large regional following in the Southeast. See the Web site listings below for contact information for most of these organizations.

State

Most states have clubs that focus on numismatic events and interests specific to the state. Again, residency in the state is usually not required for membership. See the Club Directory section of the ANA Web site for information on state numismatic organizations.

Local

Many cities large and small have local coin clubs that meet regularly. The Club Directory section of the ANA Web site can help locate a club in or near a specific city. The events listings in local newspapers may help, too.

Special interest

Some clubs focus on a specific collecting interest, such as commemoratives, silver dollars, or coins of a particular country. They draw their membership nationally and keep in touch through a quarterly or monthly journal. They also meet at larger numismatic events, such as the ANA conventions. See the Club Directory section of the ANA Web site for listings and contact information.

SHOWS

Most numismatic organizations sponsor conventions and shows as part of their activities. They range from multi-day events with a national or even world focus, such as the ANA's annual conventions, to smaller one-day events sponsored by the local coin club.

The events usually include a bourse, an area where dealers set-up to buy and sell coins. The local events may have a couple of dozen dealers; the larger events can have hundreds of dealers and booths for the U.S. Mint and other world mints. Both, however, give collectors the chance to look at a lot of coins in one location.

The larger events also feature educational opportunities, such as competitive exhibits and seminars.

Numismatic periodicals, such as the monthly *Coins* magazine, available on many newsstands, and the weekly *Numismatic News*, list upcoming shows throughout the country. The Numismaster Web site (www.numismaster.com) and the ANA Web site also list upcoming events.

World mints participate in some larger shows, such as the ANA events.

BOOKS

The following books, all by Krause Publications, provide more information on coins and can also help novice collectors take the next step in their collecting pursuits. They are available at most bookstores, online booksellers, or directly from the publisher at www.krausebooks.com or www.shop.collect.com.

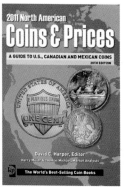

2011 North American Coins & Prices, 20th Edition

North American Coins and Prices

The bulk of this book is value listings for U.S., Canadian, and Mexican coins, but it also provides basic information on grading, how coins are made, assembling a collection, caring for coins, and market updates. New editions are published annually.

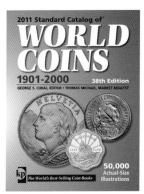

Standard Catalog of World Coins 1901-2000, 38th Edition

Standard Catalog of World Coins

This multi-volume series, published since 1972 and known worldwide, lists and values every coin produced in the world since 1601. The books are broken down by century, and each volume can be purchased individually. A three-DVD set going back to 1801 is also available.

Warman's Companion U.S. Coins & Currency, 2nd Edition

U.S. Coins & Currency

Part of the Warman's Companion series, this book provides comprehensive coverage of U.S. coins and extensive coverage of U.S. paper money, including background information on each type of note. Introductory chapters cover some basic information about collecting U.S. coins and paper money.

U.S. Coin Digest

This hardcover book with a spiral binding provides comprehensive listings and values for all U.S. coins. Introductory material covers some of the basics of coin collecting. New editions are published annually.

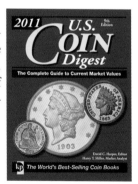

2011 U.S. Coin Digest, 9th Edition

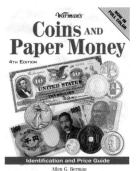

Warman's Coins & Paper Money, 4th Edition

Warman's Coins & Paper Money

Geared toward new collectors, this book is a value and identification guide for U.S., Canadian, and other world coins and paper money. The large-format book (8-1/2" x 11") contains more than 3,000 photos.

World Coins & Currency

Part of the Warman's Companion series, this book provides a good overview of world coinage and paper money. It's a lower-cost alternative to the much bigger but more comprehensive Standard Catalog of World Coins.

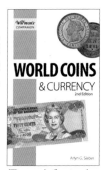

Warman's Companion World Coins & Currency, 2nd Edition

PERIODICALS

The following publications provide news and information on a wide range of numismatic topics. In addition to their editorial content, their advertising provides a shop-at-home marketplace for coins from dealers nationwide.

Coins

This monthly magazine (www.coinsmagazine.net) is available by subscription and on many newsstands. Its features and columns focus on U.S. coins, but also cover the gamut of world numismatics. A U.S. coin value guide is included in each issue.

Coin Prices

Published six times annually, *Coin Prices* magazine (www.coin-pricesmagazine.net) is a complete guide to U.S. coin values. It's available by subscription and on many newsstands.

Coin Prices magazine is published six times annually, and is available by subscription and on many newsstands.

Numismatic News

This weekly tabloid, founded in 1952, focuses on U.S. hobby news and events, but also includes features and columns covering a wide range of topics. A monthly value-guide supplement provides current listings for selected U.S. coins and market commentary and analysis. It's available by subscription and on some larger newsstands.

Numismatic News, founded in 1952, focuses on U.S. hobby news and events but also includes features and columns covering a wide range of topics. It's available by subscription and on some larger newsstands.

World Coin News

Similar in format to *Numismatic News*, the monthly *World Coin News* focuses on non-U.S. issues. It's available by subscription and on some larger newsstands.

WEB SITES

The following Web sites provide more information and resources on numismatic organizations, shows, publications, and coin collecting in general.

www.centralstates.info

Site for the Central States Numismatic Society. Provides news and information on this regional organization.

www.cmm.gob.mx

Site for the Casa de Moneda de México, Mexico's official mint.

www.coinpricesmagazine.net

Site for *Coin Prices* magazine. Includes subscription information and selected articles.

www.coinsmagazine.net

Site for *Coins* magazine. Includes subscription information, selected articles, and videos.

www.funtopics.com

Site for the Florida United Numismatists. Provides news and information on the organization.

www.krausebooks.com

Source for coin books published by Krause Publications.

www.mint.ca

Site for the Royal Canadian Mint, Canada's official mint. Includes ordering information for current issues.

www.nenacoin.com

Site for the New England Numismatic Association. Provides news and information on this regional organization.

www.numismaster.com

Sponsored by the publisher of *Numismatic News, Coins* magazine, and its related publications, the Numismaster site provides news and features, a collection management system, value guides, and more. A subscription is required to access some parts of the site.

The Numismaster site provides news and features, a collection management system, value guides, and more. A subscription is required to access some parts of the site.

www.numismaticnews.net

Site for the weekly *Numismatic News*. Includes subscription information, selected articles, and videos.

www.pnna.org

Site for the Pacific Northwest Numismatic Association. Provides news and information on this regional organization.

www.royalmint.com

Site for The Royal Mint of Great Britain, the country's official mint. Includes ordering information for current issues.

www.usmint.gov

Site for the U.S. Mint. Provides new-issue and historical information. Collectors can also order current Mint products, such as commemoratives, proof sets, and uncirculated sets.

www.worldcoinnews.net

Site for the monthly *World Coin News*. Includes subscription information, selected articles, and video.

2004-P Jefferson Nickel Peace Medal

HOW TO COLLECT MODERN U.S. COINS

A coin collection can be whatever an individual collector wants it to be. A collector may long to own just a single commemorative gold coin, for example, and a piece with a design and price the collector likes may fulfill that longing.

Traditionally, collectors pursue an example of each date-and-mintmark combination within a particular series of coins. Circulating series of modern U.S. coins are tailor-made for this traditional collecting pursuit. A complete set of circulating Westward Journey Nickels, for example, encompasses eight coins—four different designs each struck at two mints in 2004-2005—and can be completed by keeping a close watch on pocket change.

Obtaining rolls of coins from a local bank and searching for needed date-and-mintmark combinations can supplement pocket-change watches. Searching bulk quantities of coins can be particularly helpful when pursuing some of the longer modern U.S. coin series, such as the 50 State Quarters.

Coin shops, coin shows, and advertisements in coin-collecting publications like *Coin Prices* and *Numismatic News* can also be sources for modern U.S. coins, particularly for previous-years' issues in uncirculated grades. Collectors pay premiums over the coins' face values when buying through these outlets, but many of these issues are affordable, as reflected in the value listings in this book.

Whether searching circulating coinage or buying from coin dealers, the key is knowing what has been issued and what will be issued in the future. The listings in this book provide that key.

Advertisements in coin-collecting publications like Coin Prices (left) and Numismatic News (right) can be valuable sources for modern U.S. coins, particularly for previous-years' issues in uncirculated grades.

A number of the modern U.S. coins listed in this book do not circulate. These coins must be purchased directly from the U.S. Mint at the time they are issued or on the secondary market—shops, shows, and magazine advertisements—after their Mint sales period has ended.

Among them are commemorative coins. A complete collection of every commemorative half dollar, silver dollar, and gold coin issued since 1982 is a commendable but daunting goal for many collectors, especially beginners. Following are suggested strategies for collecting modern commemoratives, which can lead to expanding the collection in the future:

Collect what you like. If you see a modern commemorative coin and you like it, buy it. The coin may appeal to you because of its theme or design. Whatever the reason, if you like the coin and are willing to pay the asking price, it will make a great addition to your collection.

The 2010 Boy Scouts commemorative.

By denomination. A collector may want to focus on just the modern commemorative half dollars or the modern commemorative silver dollars. With more money to spend, a collector could also venture into gold coins and select one or more of the many commemorative gold $5 coins.

A collector can venture into gold coins and select one or more of the many commemorative gold $5 coins, like the 1997 Franklin Delano Roosevelt gold $5 coin.

By theme. Collectors of modern commemoratives can also focus on a particular theme that appeals to them, such as presidents, the Olympics or other sports, women, or military themes. Again, collect what you like.

Collectors of modern commemoratives can also focus on a particular theme that appeals to them, such as the Olympics.

Some collectors seek sets from their birth year or the birth years of their family members.

As a complement to a circulating-coin collection. One or more commemorative coins can complement a collection of circulating coins with similar design themes. For example, a 1993 silver dollar commemorating the 250th anniversary of Thomas Jefferson's birth can complement a collection of Westward Journey nickels.

By set. When selling a current-year commemorative series, the U.S. Mint often offers various sets containing individual coins in the series in uncirculated and proof versions. For example, the 1986 Statue of Liberty Centennial coin series consisted of a base-metal half dollar, silver dollar, and gold $5. Various sets of the series offered by the Mint that year included a two-coin set consisting of an uncirculated silver dollar and clad half dollar, a three-coin set consisting of uncirculated versions of each coin, and a six-coin set consisting of proof and uncirculated versions of each coin.

These and sets of other series can be found in their original Mint packaging on the secondary market.

A complete run of annual proof or mint sets going back to 1982 or beyond is also not a practical goal for most collectors. Thus, many focus on a few particular years or series of years.

For example, some collectors seek sets from their birth year and the birth years of their family members. They may seek sets from other years that have significance to them, such as a wedding year.

Some may also focus on sets containing a particular commemorative or other series of coins. For example, some may seek a complete collection of proof 50 State Quarters.

Some collectors focus on sets like the 50 State Quarters.

HOW TO HANDLE AND STORE COINS

A pile of coins in a coffee can or a shoebox or wrapped up in rolls is just a pile of coins. But organizing them so they can be conveniently stored in some orderly system and viewed on demand makes them a collection. It also preserves them for the long term. They're no longer subject to the wear and tear of circulation.

Many of the modern U.S. coins listed in this book can be found in circulation or purchased at low cost. Handling and storage considerations for these low-cost coins aren't as critical as they are for, say, a rare silver dollar worth thousands. Still, good collecting habits apply to all levels of the hobby.

HOW TO HANDLE COINS

The less coins are handled, the better. Dirty, oily hands—even if they appear to be clean—lead to dirty, oily coins.

Oftentimes, however, coins have to be handled, particularly when searching circulating coins or when transferring a coin to a holder. When it is necessary to handle a coin, it should be held by the edges between the thumb and forefinger. Avoid contact with the coin's obverse and reverse surfaces. Also, handle coins over a soft surface so they will not be damaged if accidentally dropped.

Collectible coins should be held between the thumb and forefinger.

SHOULD I CLEAN MY COINS?

No. Luster is an important aspect when grading certain high-end coins, but in general, a coin's grade and its corresponding value depend on the amount of wear on the coin, not how shiny it is. Cleaning—particularly home-brewed methods—is often abrasive and will damage a coin rather than improve it. There may be certain instances when it is desirable to clean a coin, but that is best left to experienced opinions as to when and how.

HOW TO STORE COINS

Folders

Cardboard folders are the most inexpensive and common form of organizing and storing a collection. They can be purchased at many hobby shops and bookstores.

They provide a spot for each date and mintmark in a particular series, thus acting as a road map for the collector. They are also compact and convenient; they take up little space on a bookshelf and can be pulled down and opened for easy viewing.

The spots for the coins consist of holes in the cardboard sized specially for the particular series covered by the folder. They are meant to be a tight fit so the coins, once inserted, won't fall out. Place the coin in the hole at an angle, so one side of the coin is in the hole. On the side of the coin sticking up, press down and toward the angled side until the coin snaps into place.

Coins collected from circulation can be stored in folders.

The process isn't always graceful; thus, some of the basic rules for handling coins have to be suspended when working with folders. But folders are still suitable for storing coins plucked from circulation.

2-by-2s

Low to moderately priced coins offered for sale at shops and shows are usually stored in cardboard holders commonly called "2-by-2s" because they are two inches square. They consist of two pieces with a clear Mylar window in the center. The coin is placed between the two pieces, which are then stapled together.

These 2-by-2 holders are also inexpensive. They are suitable for long-term storage and offer a number of advantages over the basic folder:

- The window in the holder allows both sides of the coin to be viewed.
- The entire coin is enclosed.
- The coin can be handled by the edges when inserted into the holder.

As for disadvantages:

- Storing an entire collection of a particular series takes up more space.
- The coins can be viewed only one at a time.
- Caution should be used when inserting or removing coins from the holders to make sure the staples' sharp edges don't damage the coins.
- There is no road map to the series. A separate checklist is needed.

Dealers often sell coins in 2-by-2 holders, which can be stored in specially designed boxes.

The 2-by-2 holders can be stored in long, narrow boxes specially sized to hold them. They can also be inserted into pockets in a plastic page, which can then be inserted into a three-ring binder.

Originally the plastic pages contained polyvinylchloride, which produced a soft, flexible pocket. But the substance breaks down over time, resulting in a green slime that could contact the coins. Manufacturers then started substituting Mylar for the PVC. The Mylar does not break down, but the page containing it is more brittle and not as flexible.

Flips

Similar in size to the cardboard 2-by-2s, plastic "flips," to use the common vernacular, are another common storage method for coins for sale. They consist of a plastic pocket, into which the coin is inserted, with a flap that folds down over the pocket. Coin dealers will often staple the flap shut.

Flips offer many of the same advantages as the cardboard 2-by-2s:

- Although they cost more, flips are still inexpensive.
- The entire coin is enclosed.
- Both sides of the coin can be viewed.
- The coin can be handled by the edges when inserted into the holder.

Also, they don't have to be stapled shut, thus eliminating the possibility of the staples scratching the coin.

Plastic "flips" are another common storage method for coins sold at coin shops.

The big disadvantage to flips is their composition. They, too, originally contained polyvinylchloride. Manufacturers then started making flips containing Mylar, but the resulting product again is more brittle and not as flexible as the old PVC flips. For long-term storage, it's best to remove coins from flips and transfer them to another type of holder.

Albums

Coin albums are a step up from the basic folder. They are in book form and contain a hole for each date and mintmark in the particular series covered. The hole has a clear plastic back and a clear plastic front. The plastic front slides out, and the coin can be placed in the hole. The plastic front is then slid back over the hole.

Albums combine many of the advantages of 2-by-2s and folders:

- They are compact and convenient, and can be stored on a bookshelf.
- They are affordable.
- Both sides of the coin can be viewed.
- Their labeled holes act as a road map to a series.
- The entire coin is enclosed.
- The coin can be handled by the edges when inserted.

The disadvantage to albums is that sliding the plastic front can damage a coin in the holder if the plastic rubs against the coin. Thus, albums are not recommended for expensive uncirculated coins.

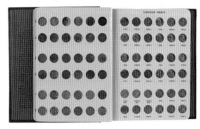

Coin albums protect both sides of a coin but also allow both sides to be viewed.

Hard-plastic holders

Hard-plastic holders are the top of the line in coin shortage but are still affordable. They consist of two pieces with one or more clear windows through which the coin or a set of coins can be viewed. The two pieces are held together with plastic screws or snap together.

To insert a coin into the holder, the two pieces are separated and the coin is placed face up into the bottom piece. The top piece is then placed over the bottom piece, and the two pieces are screwed or snapped together again.

Some of the world's great numismatic rarities are stored in hard-plastic holders. They offer all of the advantages of the less expensive storage methods but in a safe, inert environment.

Hard-plastic holders are the top of the line in coin storage.

Slabs

In 1986, a group of coin dealers got together and formed the Professional Coin Grading Service. For a fee, dealers and collectors could submit coins to the service and receive a professional opinion on their grades. After grading, a coin is encapsulated in an inert hard-plastic holder with a serial number and the service's opinion on its grade indicated on the holder.

The concept was successful, and several competing services were established in succeeding years. Today, most coins valuable enough to justify the grading fee have been graded by one of the services and encapsulated in its holder.

The grading-service holders are common at coin shows and shops, and acquired the nickname "slabs." The holders are suitable for long-term storage of high-end collectible coins.

The Professional Coin Grading Service was the first grading service to encapsulate coins after grading.

Other grading services followed PCGS' lead in encapsulating coins after grading.

STATE OF THE MARKET

Collectors who rescue 50 State Quarters, Westward Journey Nickels, or Lincoln Bicentennial Cents from circulation need not worry about fluctuations in the numismatic market. Their investment is the coins' face value, and it's unlikely the coins will appreciate in value in the future.

Those, however, who venture into modern issues containing gold or silver—such as commemoratives and bullion coins—should pay closer attention to some of the factors that affect secondary-market values.

Precious metal content provides the base value for any gold or silver coin. For example, modern commemorative silver dollars contain .76 troy ounces of silver—the same as circulating silver dollars of the 1800s and early 1900s. So if silver is selling for $15 a troy ounce, a modern commemorative silver dollar will be worth at least $11.40 (15 x .76).

Gold and silver coins with collectible or numismatic value sell for a premium above their precious-metal value. The extent of the premium depends on the coin's grade, its rarity, and the demand for the coin in the collector market. As shown in the value listings in this book, many commemorative coins that sold poorly when first issued by the U.S. Mint are worth more today than coins that sold well. The poor sales resulted in low mintages, which resulted in rarity, which resulted in increased demand for the coins on the secondary market. (Collectors, however, should be aware that rarity doesn't always mean increased demand in the numismatic market.)

Premiums over precious-metal content can vary from a few percentage points for bullion coins to several hundred percent for high-quality or rare collectible coins. If the premium is high, the coin is not affected as much by fluctuating market prices for silver and gold bullion. If the premium is low, the coin's value is more likely to be affected by the ups and downs of the bullion markets.

Local coin dealers base their prices on world bullion markets when buying and selling precious-metals coins. The benchmark price per troy ounce worldwide is the twice-daily fixings of the London Bullion Market Association. The fixings allow association market participants to buy and sell large quantities of gold and silver over the counter at a single quoted price. They also provide a reference price for many small, private transactions at local outlets, such as coin shops. Many trades worldwide are settled at the London p.m. fix.

In New York, gold and silver trade daily on the New York Mercantile Exchange. "New York spot" is the price at which gold or silver is trading at any given moment during normal trading hours, and is another way to determine the value of a coin containing a precious metal. "New York close," or the day's last price, is also a benchmark for some gold and silver trades.

Gold and silver prices rode a roller coaster during the recent economic turmoil. Gold averaged $968 a troy ounce in March 2008 before falling to an average of $760 a troy ounce in November 2008. It closed the year at about $870.

It rose to about $950 a troy ounce in mid-2009 before topping $1,000 by year's end. It was trading at more than $1,200 a troy ounce by mid-2010.

Silver topped $20 a troy ounce in March 2008 before ending the year at $10.79. It rose steadily in 2009, topping $18 a troy ounce in November before ending the year at about $17. It was back over the $18 mark by mid-2010.

As a result, values for gold and silver coins rode the same roller coaster during this time and will likewise be affected by any future fluctuations in bullion prices.

A number of Web sites and financial news services publish the London fixings and New York spot prices throughout the trading day as well as historical charts and data. Precious-metals prices also are published in most daily newspapers.

Factors that can affect the prices of gold and silver include supply, demand, the rate of inflation, the U.S. dollar's value against other major currencies, local and international economic conditions, and major world events. Because gold is priced in U.S. dollars on world markets, it often, though not always, has an inverse relationship to the dollar's value. If the dollar rises against other major currencies, the price of gold tends to fall. Conversely, if the dollar decreases in value, gold often rises.

ABOUT THE VALUE LISTINGS

Coin values listed in this book are estimated retail prices. These are the approximate prices collectors can expect to pay when buying the listed coins in the listed grades from dealers at shows and shops, and through advertisements in coin-collecting magazines.

Four grades of condition are used in the listings:

(1) Unc. This generic uncirculated grade is used for bullion coins, like the various American Eagle issues, whose values are primarily determined by their bullion content and the current price for the precious metal they contain. Uncirculated bullion coins should show no wear in their designs, as circulating coins do, but they may have varying degrees of original luster and blemishes such as contact marks (marks obtained when the coins bang against each other during shipment), hairline scratches, and scuff marks.

(2) MS-63. This is also an uncirculated grade ("MS" means "mint state"), but according to the American Numismatic Association's official grading standards, an MS-63 coin may have "slightly impaired" luster, "numerous small contact marks," and a "few scattered heavy marks." "Several detracting scuff marks or defects may be present throughout the design or in the fields," the standards say. "The general quality is about average, but overall the coin is rather attractive."

(3) MS-65. A higher standard of uncirculated, an MS-65 coin is "above average and eye appeal is very pleasing," according to the ANA guidelines. A few small, scattered contact marks may be present, and one or two "small patches of hairlines" may show. "Noticeable light scuff marks may be seen on the high points of the design," the ANA standards say.

(4) Proof-65. "Proof" describes a process of manufacture rather than a grade. Proof coins are struck from specially selected, highly polished planchets and dies. They usually receive multiple strikes from the coining press at increased pressure. The result is a coin with mirror-like surfaces and, in recent years, a cameo effect on its raised design surfaces.

The coins are then carefully handled; placed in sealed, inert holders; and sold to collectors in sets. Like other coins, however, proof coins can come in varying degrees of condition. Thus, there are various grade designations for proofs, but the coins are always termed "proofs."

A proof-65 coin shows an "attractive high quality of mirror surface," according to the ANA standards. "A few small scattered contact marks, or two larger marks, may be present, and hairlines may show under magnification," the standards say. "The eye appeal is above average and very pleasing for the variety."

Except for the bullion issues, modern coins sold by dealers in uncirculated grades usually were originally purchased from the U.S. Mint in officially issued uncirculated sets. The sets were then broken up so the coins could be sold individually. It is unlikely that a coin found in circulation will meet the standards for uncirculated grades.

Examples of coins listed in this book and found in circulation are usually worth their face value only. That should not, however, discourage anyone from collecting these coins from circulation. Collecting from circulation has been a staple of coin collecting for decades. That's how many of today's veteran collectors got started.

The dates in the value listings are the dates on the coins. A letter following the date is the mintmark on the coin. The mintmark indicates which U.S. Mint facility struck the coin. The following mintmarks appear on modern U.S. coins:

P – Philadelphia Mint. Often referred to as the "main" U.S. mint, the Philadelphia Mint strikes all denominations of circulating coins and some commemorative coins. Circulating coins without mintmarks were also struck at Philadelphia except for some one-cent coins of 1973-1986, which were struck at West Point.

D – Denver Mint. The Denver Mint produces all denominations of circulating coins and has also struck some modern commemoratives.

S – San Francisco Mint. The San Francisco Mint produces proof coins only.

W – West Point Mint. Located in West Point, N.Y., this facility was built in 1937 as the West Point Bullion Depository. It produced one-cent coins without a mintmark from 1973-1986. It was officially designated a U.S. branch mint in 1988. Its "W" mintmark first appeared on the 1986 State of Liberty Centennial commemorative gold $5 coin. All of the American Eagle bullion coins—proof and uncirculated—are produced at West Point along with some commemoratives.

A dash under a grade heading in the value listings means either a secondary market for the coin had not been established by the time this book went to press or the date and mintmark combination listed was not produced in either uncirculated or proof version. For example, the San Francisco Mint produces only proof coins, so there are no value listings for S-mintmarked coins under the uncirculated grade headings.

For more on grading coins, see the book "The American Numismatic Association Grading Standards for United States Coins," available through the ANA's Web site at www.money.org.

The current San Francisco Mint.

LINCOLN BICENTENNIAL CENTS (2009)

Title III of the Presidential $1 Coin Act of 2005 directed the U.S. Mint to issue four different circulating one-cent coins in 2009 to commemorate the bicentennial of Abraham Lincoln's birth. The law directed that the Victor David Brenner bust of Lincoln continue on the obverses of the new coins. It was introduced on the cent in 1909 to mark the centennial of the 16th president's birth and was used ever since. It further directed that four different reverses be released at quarterly intervals during the year. The first reverse was to be emblematic of Lincoln's birth and early childhood in Kentucky; the second, his formative years in Indiana; the third, his professional life in Illinois; and the fourth, his presidency.

Reverse design for the first coin, released Jan. 12, 2009, depicts a log cabin with Lincoln's birth year, 1809, below. The second reverse design, released May 14, 2009, shows a young Lincoln sitting on a log reading a book with an ax at his side. Lincoln loved to read and often took a book with him to read during breaks in his work on his family's southern Indiana farm.

The third reverse, released Aug. 13, 2009, shows Lincoln standing in front of what is now the Old State Capitol in Springfield, Ill. Lincoln was elected to the Illinois General Assembly in 1834, earned his law license in 1836, and was elected to the U.S. House of Representatives in 1846. The fourth reverse, released Nov. 12, 2009, shows the U.S. Capitol with its dome half finished. The design symbolizes the nation torn apart by the Civil War during Lincoln's presidency. The current Capitol dome was still under construction when Lincoln was first inaugurated in 1861. It was completed in 1863, and Lincoln's body lay in state under the dome after he died on April 15, 1865.

Lincoln Bicentennial cents struck for circulation contain the predominately zinc composition used for circulating cents since 1982. The law authorizing the bicentennial coins also stipulated that the Mint issue the coins in a predominately copper composition for "numismatic purposes." The copper versions use the same specifications as the original Lincoln cent in 1909 and were struck in proof and uncirculated versions for sale to collectors.

Beginning in 2010, the Lincoln-cent reverse design symbolized Lincoln's preservation of the United States as a single, unified country. The design chosen shows a union shield with a scroll draped across it bearing the inscription "E Pluribus Unum."

The authorizing law further stipulated that beginning in 2010, the Lincoln-cent reverse design should symbolize Lincoln's preservation of the United States as a single, unified country. The design chosen shows a union shield with a scroll draped across it bearing the inscription "E Pluribus Unum."

Diameter: 19 millimeters. **Weight:** 2.5 grams (zinc composition) and 3.11 grams (copper composition). **Copper-plated zinc composition:** 97.5-percent zinc, 2.5-percent copper. **Copper composition:** 95-percent copper, 5-percent tin and zinc.

2009 Lincoln Cent (obverse)

Log Cabin			
Date	Mintage	MS-65	Proof-65
2009-P zinc	284,400,000	1.50	—
2009-P copper	—	1.50	—
2009-D zinc	350,400,000	1.50	—
2009-D copper	—	1.50	—
2009-S copper	—	—	4.00

2009 Lincoln Cent (Log Cabin)

Lincoln Reading

Date	Mintage	MS-65	Proof-65
2009-P zinc	376,000,000	1.50	—
2009-P copper	—	1.50	—
2009-D zinc	363,600,000	1.50	—
2009-D copper	—	1.50	—
2009-S copper	—	—	4.00

2009 Lincoln Cent (Lincoln Reading)

Illinois Old State Capitol

Date	Mintage	MS-65	Proof-65
2009-P zinc	316,000,000	1.50	—
2009-P copper	—	1.50	—
2009-D zinc	336,000,000	1.50	—
2009-D copper	—	1.50	—
2009-S copper	—	—	4.00

2009 Lincoln Cent (Illinois Old State Capitol)

U.S. Capitol

Date	Mintage	MS-65	Proof-65
2009-P zinc	129,600,000	1.50	—
2009-P copper	—	1.50	—
2009-D zinc	198,000,000	1.50	—
2009-D copper	—	1.50	—
2009-S copper	—	—	4.00

2009 Lincoln Cent (U.S. Capitol)

WESTWARD JOURNEY NICKEL SERIES (2004-2005)

The two-year Westward Journey Nickel Series commemorated the bicentennial of Lewis and Clark's exploration of the Louisiana Territory. President Thomas Jefferson authorized the mission to find the "most direct & practicable water communication across this continent for the purpose of commerce."

The series' 2004 issues paired the traditional bust of Jefferson used on the nickel since 1938 with two different reverse designs. The first reverse was based on the original design for an Indian peace medal commissioned for Lewis and Clark's expedition. It depicts two clasped hands. The wrist of one hand is adorned with the cuff of a military uniform; the wrist of the other hand is adorned with beads and a stylized American eagle. The design was meant to symbolize friendship between the American government and the Native Americans that Lewis and Clark would encounter on their exploration. The explorers carried the medals with them and gave them to Native American leaders as a goodwill gesture.

The second 2004 reverse depicts a keelboat—the watercraft Lewis and Clark used in their expedition. The two uniformed figures in the boat's bow represent the two explorers.

For 2005, a new depiction of Jefferson on the obverse was paired with two more new reverses – an American bison and a view of the Pacific Ocean. The bison design is reminiscent of the so-called Buffalo nickel (1913-1938). The animal is mentioned in Lewis and Clark's journals.

The Pacific Ocean view includes the inscription "Ocean in view! Oh the joy!" The design was inspired by a Nov. 7, 1805, entry in William Clark's journal: "We are in view of the opening of the Ocean, which Creates great joy." The design is based on a photograph by Andrew E. Cier of Astoria, Ore.

Diameter: 21.2 millimeters. **Weight:** 5 grams. **Composition:** Copper-nickel.

2005-P Westward Journey Nickel (obverse)

Peace Medal			
Date	Mintage	MS-65	Proof-65
2004-P	361,440,000	1.00	—
2004-D	372,000,000	1.00	—
2004-S	—	—	13.00

2004-P Westward Journey Nickel (Peace Medal)

Keelboat

Date	Mintage	MS-65	Proof-65
2004-P	366,720,000	1.00	—
2004-D	344,880,000	1.00	—
2004-S	—	—	13.00

2004-P Westward Journey Nickel (Keelboat)

Bison

Date	Mintage	MS-65	Proof-65
2005-P	448,320,000	1.00	—
2005-D	487,680,000	1.00	—
2005-S	—	—	7.50

2005-D Westward Journey Nickel (Bison)

"Ocean in view!"

Date	Mintage	MS-65	Proof-65
2005-P	394,080,000	1.00	—
2005-D	411,120,000	1.00	—
2005-S	—	—	6.50

2005-P Westward Journey Nickel ("Ocean in view!")

50 STATE QUARTERS (1999-2008)

President Bill Clinton signed the 50 States Commemorative Coin Program Act into law on Dec. 1, 1997. The act was designed to "honor the unique Federal republic of 50 States that comprise the United States" and to "promote the diffusion of knowledge among the youth of the United States about the individual States, their history and geography, and the rich diversity of the national heritage."

Each year during the series' run, five new reverse designs were introduced on the quarter. Each design honored a different state in the order in which each state ratified the Constitution or were admitted to the union. The bust of Washington used on the quarter since 1932 was retained on the obverse.

The law authorizing the coins banned any "frivolous or inappropriate design" and prohibited the depiction of a head-and-shoulders bust of any person living or dead, or any representation of a living person. To accommodate the reverse designs, the words "United States of America" were moved from the quarter's reverse to the obverse, and the date was moved from the obverse to the reverse.

The law gave the U.S. Treasury secretary final design approval, but it required the secretary to consult with the states' governors on their respective designs.

The law also authorized the U.S. Mint to produce uncirculated, proof, and 90-percent-silver versions of the 50 State Quarters for sale to collectors.

Beginning in 2005, coins in the U.S. Mint's annual uncirculated sets have been produced with a satin finish to distinguish them from uncirculated business strikes. As noted in the value listings, some dates with the satin finish command a premium over the business strikes in the same grade.

Diameter: 24.3 millimeters. **Weight:** 5.67 grams (clad composition) and 6.25 grams (silver composition). **Clad composition:** Layers of 75-percent copper and 25-percent nickel bonded to a pure-copper core. **Silver composition:** 90-percent silver, 10-percent copper. **Total silver weight:** .1808 troy ounces.

50 State Quarters (obverse)

Delaware

Date	Mintage	MS-63	MS-65	Proof-65
1999-P	373,400,000	1.40	8.00	—
1999-D	401,424,000	1.25	20.00	—
1999-S	3,713,359	—	—	12.00
1999-S silver	804,565	—	—	65.00

Delaware (1999)

Pennsylvania

Date	Mintage	MS-63	MS-65	Proof-65
1999-P	349,000,000	1.00	15.00	—
1999-D	358,332,000	1.00	20.00	—
1999-S	3,713,359	—	—	12.00
1999-S silver	804,565	—	—	65.00

Pennsylvania (1999)

New Jersey

Date	Mintage	MS-63	MS-65	Proof-65
1999-P	363,200,000	1.00	10.00	—
1999-D	299,028,000	1.00	9.00	—
1999-S	3,713,359	—	—	12.00
1999-S silver	804,565	—	—	65.00

New Jersey (1999)

Georgia

Date	Mintage	MS-63	MS-65	Proof-65
1999-P	451,188,000	1.20	14.00	—
1999-D	488,744,000	1.20	14.00	—
1999-S	3,713,359	—	—	12.00
1999-S silver	804,565	—	—	65.00

Georgia (1999)

Connecticut

Date	Mintage	MS-63	MS-65	Proof-65
1999-P	688,744,000	1.00	10.00	—
1999-D	657,480,000	1.00	9.00	—
1999-S	3,713,359	—	—	12.00
1999-S silver	804,565	—	—	65.00

Connecticut (1999)

Massachusetts

Date	Mintage	MS-63	MS-65	Proof-65
2000-P	629,800,000	1.00	10.00	—
2000-D	535,184,000	1.00	12.00	—
2000-S	4,078,747	—	—	3.50
2000-S silver	965,921	—	—	5.50

Massachusetts (2000)

Maryland

Date	Mintage	MS-63	MS-65	Proof-65
2000-P	678,200,000	1.00	11.00	—
2000-D	556,526,000	1.00	11.00	—
2000-S	4,078,747	—	—	3.50
2000-S silver	965,921	—	—	5.50

Maryland (2000)

South Carolina

Date	Mintage	MS-63	MS-65	Proof-65
2000-P	742,756,000	1.40	9.00	—
2000-D	566,208,000	1.40	12.00	—
2000-S	4,078,747	—	—	3.50
2000-S silver	965,921	—	—	5.50

South Carolina (2000)

New Hampshire				
Date	Mintage	MS-63	MS-65	Proof-65
2000-P	673,040,000	1.00	12.50	—
2000-D	495,976,000	1.00	10.00	—
2000-S	4,078,747	—	—	3.50
2000-S silver	965,921	—	—	5.50

New Hampshire (2000)

Virginia

Date	Mintage	MS-63	MS-65	Proof-65
2000-P	943,000,000	1.00	8.00	—
2000-D	651,616,000	1.00	8.00	
2000-S	4,078,747	—	—	3.50
2000-S silver	965,921	—	—	5.50

Virginia (2000)

New York

Date	Mintage	MS-63	MS-65	Proof-65
2001-P	655,400,000	1.00	8.50	—
2001-D	619,640,000	1.00	8.50	—
2001-S	3,009,800	—	—	11.00
2001-S silver	849,600	—	—	24.00

New York (2001)

North Carolina

Date	Mintage	MS-63	MS-65	Proof-65
2001-P	627,600,000	1.00	7.50	—
2001-D	427,876,000	1.00	8.50	—
2001-S	3,009,800	—	—	11.00
2001-S silver	849,600	—	—	22.00

North Carolina (2001)

Rhode Island

Date	Mintage	MS-63	MS-65	Proof-65
2001-P	423,000,000	1.00	6.50	—
2001-D	447,100,000	1.00	8.00	—
2001-S	3,009,800	—	—	11.00
2001-S silver	849,600	—	—	19.00

Rhode Island (2001)

Vermont

Date	Mintage	MS-63	MS-65	Proof-65
2001-P	423,400,000	1.20	7.00	—
2001-D	459,404,000	1.00	7.00	—
2001-S	3,009,800	—	—	11.00
2001-S silver	849,600	—	—	19.00

Vermont (2001)

Kentucky

Date	Mintage	MS-63	MS-65	Proof-65
2001-P	353,000,000	1.20	7.00	—
2001-D	370,564,000	1.00	8.00	—
2001-S	3,009,800	—	—	11.00
2001-S silver	849,500	—	—	21.00

Kentucky (2001)

Tennessee

Date	Mintage	MS-63	MS-65	Proof-65
2002-P	361,600,000	1.40	6.50	—
2002-D	286,468,000	1.40	7.00	—
2002-S	3,084,185	—	—	4.50
2002-S silver	892,229	—	—	9.00

Tennessee (2002)

Ohio

Date	Mintage	MS-63	MS-65	Proof-65
2002-P	217,200,000	1.00	6.50	—
2002-D	414,832,000	1.00	7.00	—
2002-S	3,084,185	—	—	4.50
2002-S silver	892,229	—	—	9.00

Ohio (2002)

Louisiana

Date	Mintage	MS-63	MS-65	Proof-65
2002-P	362,000,000	1.00	6.50	—
2002-D	402,204,000	1.00	7.00	—
2002-S	3,084,185	—	—	4.50
2002-S silver	892,229	—	—	9.00

Louisiana (2002)

Indiana

Date	Mintage	MS-63	MS-65	Proof-65
2002-P	362,600,000	1.00	6.00	—
2002-D	327,200,000	1.00	6.50	—
2002-S	3,084,185	—	—	4.50
2002-S silver	892,229	—	—	9.00

Indiana (2002)

Mississippi

Date	Mintage	MS-63	MS-65	Proof-65
2002-P	290,000,000	1.00	5.00	—
2002-D	289,600,000	1.00	6.00	—
2002-S	3,084,185	—	—	4.50
2002-S silver	892,229	—	—	9.00

Mississippi (2002)

Illinois				
Date	Mintage	MS-63	MS-65	Proof-65
2003-P	225,800,000	1.10	7.00	—
2003-D	237,400,000	1.10	6.00	—
2003-S	3,270,603	—	—	3.50
2003-S silver	—	—	—	5.25

Illinois (2003)

Alabama

Date	Mintage	MS-63	MS-65	Proof-65
2003-P	225,000,000	1.00	7.00	—
2003-D	232,400,000	1.00	7.00	—
2003-S	3,270,603	—	—	3.50
2003-S silver	—	—	—	5.25

Alabama (2003)

Maine

Date	Mintage	MS-63	MS-65	Proof-65
2003-P	217,400,000	1.00	6.50	—
2003-D	213,400,000	1.00	8.00	—
2003-S	3,270,603	—	—	3.50
2003-S silver	—	—	—	5.25

Maine (2003)

Missouri

Date	Mintage	MS-63	MS-65	Proof-65
2003-P	225,000,000	1.00	7.00	—
2003-D	228,200,000	1.00	7.00	—
2003-S	3,270,603	—	—	3.50
2003-S silver	—	—	—	5.25

Missouri (2003)

Arkansas

Date	Mintage	MS-63	MS-65	Proof-65
2003-P	228,000,000	1.00	7.00	—
2003-D	229,800,000	1.00	7.00	—
2003-S	3,270,603	—	—	3.50
2003-S silver	—	—	—	5.25

Arkansas (2003)

Michigan

Date	Mintage	MS-63	MS-65	Proof-65
2004-P	233,800,000	.75	6.50	—
2004-D	225,800,000	.75	6.50	—
2004-S	—	—	—	5.00
2004-S silver	—	—	—	6.00

Michigan (2004)

Florida

Date	Mintage	MS-63	MS-65	Proof-65
2004-P	240,200,000	.75	6.50	—
2004-D	241,600,000	.75	7.00	—
2004-S	—	—	—	5.00
2004-S silver	—	—	—	6.00

Florida (2004)

Texas

Date	Mintage	MS-63	MS-65	Proof-65
2004-P	278,800,000	.75	7.00	—
2004-D	263,000,000	.75	7.00	—
2004-S	—	—	—	5.00
2004-S silver	—	—	—	6.00

Texas (2004)

Iowa

Date	Mintage	MS-63	MS-65	Proof-65
2004-P	213,800,000	.75	6.50	—
2004-D	251,800,000	.75	7.00	—
2004-S	—	—	—	5.00
2004-S silver	—	—	—	6.00

Iowa (2004)

Wisconsin

Date	Mintage	MS-63	MS-65	Proof-65
2004-P	226,400,000	1.00	8.00	—
2004-D	226,800,000	1.00	10.00	—
2004-S	—	—	—	5.00
2004-S silver	—	—	—	6.00

Wisconsin (2004)

Wisconsin "Extra-Leaf" Varieties

A number of 2004 Wisconsin quarters were struck with what appears to be an "extra leaf" in the ear of corn on the reverse. The "extra leaf" appears to the viewer's left of the ear of corn beneath the large turned-down leaf. Two variations of the "extra-leaf" quarters are known. On one, the "extra leaf" is pointed downward ("extra leaf low"); on the other, the "extra leaf" is pointed upward ("extra leaf high"). The varieties were caused by a faulty working die that was used to strike several thousand coins at the Denver Mint before it was removed from the coining press.

Date	Mintage	MS-63	MS-65	Proof-65
2004-D extra leaf low	9,000 (est.)	300.00	600.00	—
2004-D extra leaf high	3,000 (est.)	400.00	900.00	—

A normal Wisconsin quarter (left), the "leaf low" variety (middle), and the "leaf high" variety (right). (Photos courtesy of Ken Potter.)

California

Date	Mintage	MS-63	MS-65	Proof-65
2005-P	257,200,000	.75	5.00	—
2005-P satin finish	—	3.50	6.00	—
2005-D	263,200,000	.75	5.00	—
2005-D satin finish	—	3.50	6.00	—
2005-S	—	—	—	3.00
2005-S silver	—	—	—	5.50

California (2005)

Minnesota				
Date	Mintage	MS-63	MS-65	Proof-65
2005-P	226,400,000	.75	5.00	—
2005-P satin finish	—	3.50	6.00	—
2005-D	226,800,000	.75	5.00	—
2005-D satin finish	—	3.50	6.00	—
2005-S	—	—	—	3.00
2005-S silver	—	—	—	5.50

Minnesota (2005)

Oregon

Date	Mintage	MS-63	MS-65	Proof-65
2005-P	316,200,000	.75	5.00	—
2005-P satin finish	—	3.50	6.00	—
2005-D	404,000,000	.75	5.00	—
2005-D satin finish	—	3.50	6.00	—
2005-S	—	—	—	3.00
2005-S silver	—	—	—	5.50

Oregon (2005)

Kansas

Date	Mintage	MS-63	MS-65	Proof-65
2005-P	263,400,000	.75	5.00	—
2005-P satin finish	—	3.50	6.00	—
2005-D	300,000,000	.75	5.00	—
2005-D satin finish	—	3.50	6.00	—
2005-S	—	—	—	3.00
2005-S silver	—	—	—	5.50

Kansas (2005)

West Virginia

Date	Mintage	MS-63	MS-65	Proof-65
2005-P	365,400,000	.75	5.00	—
2005-P satin finish	—	3.50	6.00	—
2005-D	356,200,000	.75	5.00	—
2005-D satin finish	—	3.50	6.00	—
2005-S	—	—	—	3.00
2005-S silver	—	—	—	5.50

West Virginia (2005)

Nevada

Date	Mintage	MS-63	MS-65	Proof-65
2006-P	277,000,000	.75	6.00	—
2006-P satin finish	—	3.00	5.00	—
2006-D	312,800,000	.75	6.00	—
2006-D satin finish	—	3.00	5.00	—
2006-S	—	—	—	5.00
2006-S silver	—	—	—	5.75

Nevada (2006)

Nebraska

Date	Mintage	MS-63	MS-65	Proof-65
2006-P	318,000,000	.75	6.00	—
2006-P satin finish	—	3.00	5.00	—
2006-D	273,000,000	.75	6.00	—
2006-D satin finish	—	.75	6.00	—
2006-S	—	—	—	5.00
2006-S silver	—	—	—	5.75

Nebraska (2006)

Colorado

Date	Mintage	MS-63	MS-65	Proof-65
2006-P	274,800,000	.75	5.00	—
2006-P satin finish	—	3.00	5.00	—
2006-D	294,200,000	.75	5.00	—
2006-D satin finish	—	3.00	5.00	—
2006-S	—	—	—	5.00
2006-S silver	—	—	—	5.75

Colorado (2006)

North Dakota				
Date	Mintage	MS-63	MS-65	Proof-65
2006-P	305,800,000	.75	5.00	—
2006-P satin finish	—	3.00	5.00	—
2006-D	359,000,000	.75	5.00	—
2006-D satin finish	—	3.00	5.00	—
2006-S	—	—	—	5.00
2006-S silver	—	—	—	5.75

North Dakota (2006)

South Dakota

Date	Mintage	MS-63	MS-65	Proof-65
2006-P	245,000,000	.75	5.00	—
2006-P satin finish	—	3.00	5.00	—
2006-D	265,800,000	.75	5.00	—
2006-D satin finish	—	3.00	5.00	—
2006-S	—	—	—	5.00
2006-S silver	—	—	—	5.75

South Dakota (2006)

Montana

Date	Mintage	MS-63	MS-65	Proof-65
2007-P	257,000,000	.75	8.00	—
2007-D	256,240,000	.75	5.00	—
2007-S	—	—	—	4.00
2007-S silver	—	—	—	6.50

Montana (2007)

Washington

Date	Mintage	MS-63	MS-65	Proof-65
2007-P	265,200,000	.75	8.00	—
2007-D	280,000,000	.75	8.00	—
2007-S	—	—	—	4.00
2007-S silver	—	—	—	6.50

Washington (2007)

Idaho

Date	Mintage	MS-63	MS-65	Proof-65
2007-P	294,600,000	.75	8.00	—
2007-D	286,800,000	.75	8.00	—
2007-S	—	—	—	4.00
2007-S silver	—	—	—	6.50

Idaho (2007)

Wyoming

Date	Mintage	MS-63	MS-65	Proof-65
2007-P	243,600,000	.75	8.00	—
2007-D	320,800,000	.75	8.00	—
2007-S	—	—	—	4.00
2007-S silver	—	—	—	6.50

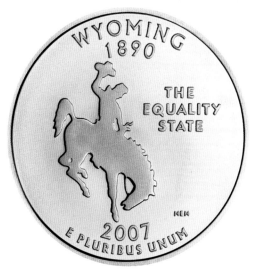

Wyoming (2007)

Utah

Date	Mintage	MS-63	MS-65	Proof-65
2007-P	255,000,000	.75	8.00	—
2007-D	253,200,000	.75	8.00	—
2007-S	—	—	—	4.00
2007-S silver	—	—	—	6.50

Utah (2007)

Oklahoma

Date	Mintage	MS-63	MS-65	Proof-65
2008-P	222,000,000	.75	8.00	—
2008-D	194,600,000	.75	8.00	—
2008-S	—	—	—	4.00
2008-S silver	—	—	—	6.50

Oklahoma (2008)

New Mexico

Date	Mintage	MS-63	MS-65	Proof-65
2008-P	244,200,000	.75	8.00	—
2008-D	244,400,000	.75	8.00	—
2008-S	—	—	—	4.00
2008-S silver	—	—	—	6.50

New Mexico (2008)

Arizona

Date	Mintage	MS-63	MS-65	Proof-65
2008-P	244,600,000	.75	8.00	—
2008-D	265,000,000	.75	8.00	—
2008-S	—	—	—	4.00
2008-S silver	—	—	—	6.50

Arizona (2008)

Alaska

Date	Mintage	MS-63	MS-65	Proof-65
2008-P	251,800,000	.75	8.00	—
2008-D	254,000,000	.75	8.00	—
2008-S	—	—	—	4.00
2008-S silver	—	—	—	6.50

Alaska (2008)

Hawaii

Date	Mintage	MS-63	MS-65	Proof-65
2008-P	254,000,000	.75	8.00	—
2008-D	263,600,000	.75	8.00	—
2008-S	—	—	—	4.50
2008-S silver	—	—	—	6.50

Hawaii (2008)

D.C. AND U.S. TERRITORIES QUARTERS (2009)

Legislation authorizing the District of Columbia and U.S. Territories Quarters was part of the 2008 Consolidated Appropriations Act, signed into law by President George W. Bush. Similar to the 50 State Quarters, the legislation required the U.S. Treasury secretary to consult with the chief executive of the District of Columbia and each of the five U.S. territories on the respective designs.

Each of the chief executives submitted two to three design narratives to the Treasury secretary. U.S. Mint designers created design proposals from the narratives. The proposals were reviewed by the Commission of Fine Arts and the Citizens Coinage Advisory Committee. The Treasury secretary had final design approval. Again, similar to the 50 State Quarters, the authorizing legislation forbade any frivolous or inappropriate design, a depiction of a living person, or a head-and-shoulders image of any person living or dead. The traditional bust of George Washington, used on the quarter since 1932, was retained for the obverse of each coin.

The coins were released in two-month intervals beginning with the District of Columbia quarter in February 2009. It was followed, in order, by the coins honoring Puerto Rico, Guam, American Samoa, U.S. Virgin Islands, and the Northern Mariana Islands.

As with the 50 State Quarters, the legislation authorized the Mint to strike uncirculated, proof, and 90-percent-silver versions for sale to collectors.

Diameter: 24.3 millimeters. **Weight:** 5.67 grams (clad composition) and 6.25 grams (silver composition). **Clad composition:** Layers of 75-percent copper and 25-percent nickel bonded to a pure-copper core. **Silver composition:** 90-percent silver, 10-percent copper. **Total silver weight:** .1808 troy ounces.

D.C. and U.S. Territories Quarters (obverse)

District of Columbia

Date	Mintage	MS-63	MS-65	Proof-65
2009-P	83,600,000	.75	8.00	—
2009-D	88,800,000	.75	8.00	—
2009-S	—	—	—	4.00
2009-S silver	—	—	—	6.50

2009 Quarter (District of Columbia)

Puerto Rico

Date	Mintage	MS-63	MS-65	Proof-65
2009-P	53,200,000	.75	8.00	—
2009-D	86,000,000	.75	8.00	—
2009-S	—	—	—	4.00
2009-S silver	—	—	—	6.50

2009 Quarter (Puerto Rico)

Guam

Date	Mintage	MS-63	MS-65	Proof-65
2009-P	53,200,000	.75	8.00	—
2009-D	42,600,000	.75	8.00	—
2009-S	—	—	—	4.00
2009-S silver	—	—	—	6.50

2009 Quarter (Guam)

American Samoa

Date	Mintage	MS-63	MS-65	Proof-65
2009-P	42,600,000	.75	8.00	—
2009-D	39,600,000	.75	8.00	—
2009-S	—	—	—	4.00
2009-S silver	—	—	—	6.50

2009 Quarter (American Samoa)

U.S. Virgin Islands				
Date	Mintage	MS-63	MS-65	Proof-65
2009-P	41,000,000	.75	8.00	—
2009-D	41,000,000	.75	8.00	—
2009-S	—	—	—	4.00
2009-S silver	—	—	—	6.50

2009 Quarter (U.S. Virgin Islands)

Northern Mariana Islands				
Date	Mintage	MS-63	MS-65	Proof-65
2009-P	35,200,000	.75	8.00	—
2009-D	37,600,000	.75	8.00	—
2009-S	—	—	—	4.00
2009-S silver	—	—	—	6.50

2009 Quarter (Northern Mariana Islands)

AMERICA THE BEAUTIFUL QUARTERS (2010-2021)

The America the Beautiful Quarters program will continue the issuance of circulating quarters with commemorative reverse designs. Five different reverse designs honoring national parks and national sites will be issued in each year from 2010-2020. The final issue in the 56-coin series is scheduled for release in 2021. Every state, U.S. territory, and the District of Columbia will be represented in the series.

The coins' authorizing legislation—America's Beautiful National Parks Quarter Dollar Coin Act of 2008—charged the U.S. Treasury secretary with selecting the sites to be honored in consultation with the Department of the Interior and the governor of each state or territory. The list of sites to be honored was announced Sept. 9, 2009.

Like legislation for the state and territories quarters, the national sites legislation prohibits a head-and-shoulders depiction of any person living or dead, or a depiction of any living person. It also prohibits an outline or map of a state in the designs. The bust of George Washington, used on the obverse of the quarter since 1932, will continue to be used on the America the Beautiful Quarters.

The legislation again authorizes the issuance of uncirculated, proof, and 90-percent-silver versions of the coins for sale to collectors.

Before the end of the series' ninth year, the Treasury secretary can decide to continue the series by honoring a second site in each state, territory, and the District of Columbia.

The legislation also authorizes the issuance of silver-bullion versions of the America the Beautiful quarters (see America the Beautiful Silver Bullion Coins). The bullion versions' designs will be exact duplicates of the circulating quarters' designs but will be 3 inches in diameter, will weigh five ounces, and will contain .999-fine silver.

Diameter: 24.3 millimeters. **Weight:** 5.67 grams (clad composition) and 6.25 grams (silver composition). **Clad composition:** Layers of 75-percent copper and 25-percent nickel bonded to a pure-copper core. **Silver composition:** 90-percent silver, 10-percent copper. **Total silver weight:** .1808 troy ounces.

America the Beautiful Quarters (obverse)

Hot Springs National Park				
Location: Arkansas. Established: 1832.				
Date	Mintage	MS-63	MS-65	Proof-65
2010-P	—	—	—	—
2010-D	—	—	—	—
2010-S	—	—	—	—
2010-S silver	—	—	—	—

2010 Quarter (Hot Springs National Park)

Yellowstone National Park Location: Wyoming. Established: 1872.				
Date	Mintage	MS-63	MS-65	Proof-65
2010-P	—	—	—	—
2010-D	—	—	—	—
2010-S	—	—	—	—
2010-S silver	—	—	—	—

2010 Quarter (Yellowstone National Park)

Yosemite National Park
Location: California. Established: 1890.

Date	Mintage	MS-63	MS-65	Proof-65
2010-P	—	—	—	—
2010-D	—	—	—	—
2010-S	—	—	—	—
2010-S silver	—	—	—	—

2010 Quarter (Yosemite National Park)

Grand Canyon National Park Location: Arizona. Established: 1893.				
Date	Mintage	MS-63	MS-65	Proof-65
2010-P	—	—	—	—
2010-D	—	—	—	—
2010-S	—	—	—	—
2010-S silver	—	—	—	—

2010 Quarter (Grand Canyon National Park)

Mount Hood National Forest
Location: Oregon. Established: 1893.

Date	Mintage	MS-63	MS-65	Proof-65
2010-P	—	—	—	—
2010-D	—	—	—	—
2010-S	—	—	—	—
2010-S silver	—	—	—	—

2010 Quarter (Mount Hood National Forest)

	Location	Site	Est.
2011	Pennsylvania	Gettysburg National Military Park	1895
	Montana	Glacier National Park	1897
	Washington	Olympic National Park	1897
	Mississippi	Vicksburg National Military Park	1899
	Oklahoma	Chickasaw National Recreation Area	1902
2012	Puerto Rico	El Yunque National Forest	1903
	New Mexico	Chaco Culture National Historical Park	1907
	Maine	Acadia National Park	1916
	Hawaii	Hawai'i Volcanoes National Park	1916
	Alaska	Denali National Park	1917
2013	New Hampshire	White Mountain National Forest	1918
	Ohio	Perry's Victory and International Peace Memorial	1919
	Nevada	Great Basin National Park	1922
	Maryland	Fort McHenry National Monument and Historic Shrine	1925
	South Dakota	Mount Rushmore National Memorial	1925
2014	Tennessee	Great Smoky Mountains National Park	1926
	Virginia	Shenandoah National Park	1926
	Utah	Arches National Park	1929
	Colorado	Great Sand Dunes National Park	1932
	Florida	Everglades National Park	1934

	Location	Site	Est.
2015	Nebraska	Homestead National Monument of America	1936
	Louisiana	Kisatchie National Forest	1936
	North Carolina	Blue Ridge Parkway	1936
	Delaware	Bombay Hook National Wildlife Refuge	1937
	New York	Saratoga National Historical Park	1938
2016	Illinois	Shawnee National Forest	1939
	Kentucky	Cumberland Gap National Historical Park	1940
	West Virginia	Harpers Ferry National Historical Park	1944
	North Dakota	Theodore Roosevelt National Park	1946
	South Carolina	Fort Moultrie (Fort Sumter National Monument)	1948
2017	Iowa	Effigy Mounds National Monument	1949
	District of Columbia	Frederick Douglass National Historic Site	1962
	Missouri	Ozark National Scenic Riverways	1964
	New Jersey	Ellis Island National Monument (Statue of Liberty)	1965
	Indiana	George Rogers Clark National Historical Park	1966

	Location	Site	Est.
2018	Michigan	Pictured Rocks National Lakeshore	1966
	Wisconsin	Apostle Islands National Lakeshore	1970
	Minnesota	Voyageurs National Park	1971
	Georgia	Cumberland Island National Seashore	1972
	Rhode Island	Block Island National Wildlife Refuge	1973
2019	Massachusetts	Lowell National Historical Park	1978
	Northern Mariana Islands	American Memorial Park	1978
	Guam	War in the Pacific National Historical Park	1978
	Texas	San Antonio Missions National Historical Park	1978
	Idaho	Frank Church-River of No Return Wilderness	1980
2020	American Samoa	National Park of American Samoa	1988
	Connecticut	Weir Farm National Historic Site	1990
	U.S. Virgin Islands	Salt River Bay National Historical Park and Ecological Preserve	1992
	Vermont	Marsh-Billings-Rockefeller National Historical Park	1992
	Kansas	Tallgrass Prairie National Preserve	1996
2021	Alabama	Tuskegee Airmen National Historic Site	1998

PRESIDENTIAL DOLLARS (2007-2016)

The Presidential Dollars series is yet another attempt to get Americans to use dollar coins instead of dollar bills. Although coins are more expensive to produce, they last longer than paper money, thus saving the government money in the long run.

The authorizing legislation—the Presidential $1 Coin Act of 2005—cites a Government Accountability Office study that says Americans would use dollar coins if they were struck with attractive, educational, and rotating designs, like the 50 State Quarters. The law mandates that federal agencies and agencies that receive federal funds, such as some transit authorities, take the necessary steps to ensure that they are capable of receiving and dispensing the coins.

Four presidents will be honored each year through 2015 in the order in which they served. The program is scheduled to conclude in 2016 with issues honoring Richard M. Nixon and Gerald Ford. The law specifies that a former or current president cannot be added to the series while he is still alive or within two years of his death.

The law mandates that the coins' obverses are to depict a likeness of the president being honored, his name, a number indicating the order in which he served, and the years of his term or terms. Grover Cleveland, the only president to serve two non-consecutive terms (1885-1889 and 1893-1897), is scheduled to appear on two separate coins in 2012 as the 22nd and 24th president.

The law designates that the common reverse design be a depiction of the Statue of Liberty.

Common reverse for the Presidential Dollars.

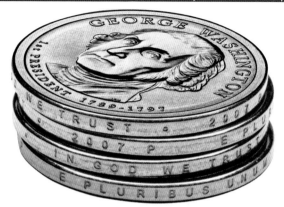

Edge lettering on Presidential Dollars.

To make more room for the obverse and reverse designs, the original law specified that each coin's date of issue, its mintmark, and the mottos "E Pluribus Unum" and "In God We Trust" appear as incused lettering on the edge. A 2007 amendment requires that "In God We Trust" appear on the coins' obverse or reverse. "In God We Trust" appears on the obverse of the Presidential Dollars beginning with the 2009 issues.

In 2007, the Mint mistakenly struck some George Washington dollars without the edge lettering. Some 2007-P John Adams dollars were struck with the edge lettering doubled.

Presidential Dollars are struck in the same specifications as the Sacagawea dollars, which have been produced since 2000 and will continue to be produced in addition to the Presidential Dollars. Uncirculated and proof versions of the Presidential Dollars are also being produced for sale to collectors.

Diameter: 26.4 millimeters. **Weight:** 8.07 grams. **Composition:** 88.5-percent copper, 6-percent zinc, 3.5-percent manganese, 2-percent nickel.

George Washington				
Date	Mintage	MS-63	MS-65	Proof-65
2007-P	176,680,000	2.00	5.00	—
2007-D	163,680,000	2.00	5.00	—
(2007) no edge lettering	—	75.00	—	—
2007-S	—	—	—	8.00

2007 Presidential Dollar (George Washington)

John Adams

Date	Mintage	MS-63	MS-65	Proof-65
2007-P	112,420,000	2.00	5.00	—
2007-D	Inc. above	250.00	—	—
(2007) no edge lettering	112,140,000	2.00	5.00	—
2007-S	—	—	—	8.00

2007 Presidential Dollar (John Adams)

Thomas Jefferson

Date	Mintage	MS-63	MS-65	Proof-65
2007-P	100,800,000	2.00	5.00	—
2007-D	102,810,000	2.00	5.00	—
2007-S	—	—	—	8.00

2007 Presidential Dollar (Thomas Jefferson)

James Madison

Date	Mintage	MS-63	MS-65	Proof-65
2007-P	84,560,000	2.00	5.00	—
2007-D	87,780,000	2.00	5.00	—
2007-S	—	—	—	8.00

2007 Presidential Dollar (James Madison)

James Monroe

Date	Mintage	MS-63	MS-65	Proof-65
2008-P	64,260,000	2.00	5.00	—
2008-D	60,230,000	2.00	5.00	—
2008-S	—	—	—	8.00

2008 Presidential Dollar (James Monroe)

John Quincy Adams

Date	Mintage	MS-63	MS-65	Proof-65
2008-P	57,540,000	2.00	5.00	—
2008-D	57,720,000	2.00	5.00	—
2008-S	—	—	—	8.00

2008 Presidential Dollar (John Quincy Adams)

Andrew Jackson

Date	Mintage	MS-63	MS-65	Proof-65
2008-P	61,180,000	2.00	5.00	—
2008-D	61,070,000	2.00	5.00	—
2008-S	—	—	—	8.00

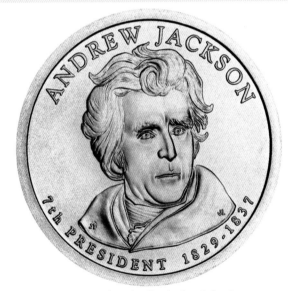

2008 Presidential Dollar (Andrew Jackson)

Martin Van Buren

Date	Mintage	MS-63	MS-65	Proof-65
2008-P	51,520,000	2.00	5.00	—
2008-D	50,960,00	2.00	5.00	—
2008-S	—	—	—	8.00

2008 Presidential Dollar (Martin Van Buren)

William Henry Harrison

Date	Mintage	MS-63	MS-65	Proof-65
2009-P	43,260,000	2.00	5.00	—
2009-D	55,160,000	2.00	5.00	—
2009-S	—	—	—	8.00

2009 Presidential Dollar (William Henry Harrison)

John Tyler

Date	Mintage	MS-63	MS-65	Proof-65
2009-P	43,540,000	2.00	5.00	—
2009-D	43,540,000	2.00	5.00	—
2009-S	—	—	—	8.00

2009 Presidential Dollar (John Tyler)

James K. Polk

Date	Mintage	MS-63	MS-65	Proof-65
2009-P	46,620,000	2.00	5.00	—
2009-D	41,720,000	2.00	5.00	—
2009-S	—	—	—	8.00

2009 Presidential Dollar (James K. Polk)

Zachary Taylor

Date	Mintage	MS-63	MS-65	Proof-65
2009-P	41,580,000	2.00	5.00	—
2009-D	36,680,000	2.00	5.00	—
2009-S	—	—	—	8.00

2009 Presidential Dollar (Zachary Taylor)

Millard Fillmore

Date	Mintage	MS-63	MS-65	Proof-65
2010-P	—	—	—	—
2010-D	—	—	—	—
2010-S	—	—	—	—

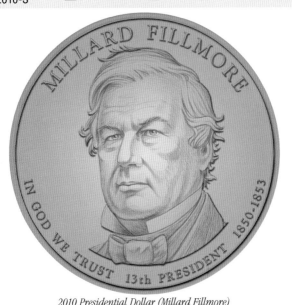

2010 Presidential Dollar (Millard Fillmore)

Franklin Pierce

Date	Mintage	MS-63	MS-65	Proof-65
2010-P	—	—	—	—
2010-D	—	—	—	—
2010-S	—	—	—	—

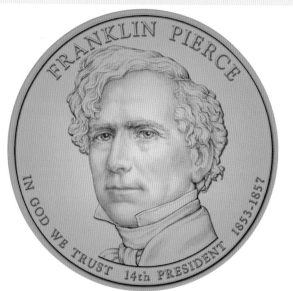

2010 Presidential Dollar (Franklin Pierce)

James Buchanan

Date	Mintage	MS-63	MS-65	Proof-65
2010-P	—	—	—	—
2010-D	—	—	—	—
2010-S	—	—	—	—

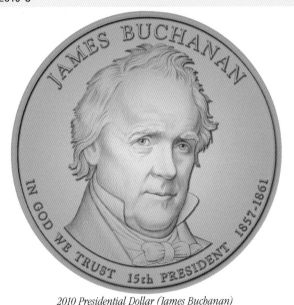

2010 Presidential Dollar (James Buchanan)

Abraham Lincoln

Date	Mintage	MS-63	MS-65	Proof-65
2010-P	—	—	—	—
2010-D	—	—	—	—
2010-S	—	—	—	—

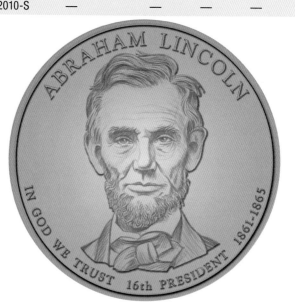

2010 Presidential Dollar (Abraham Lincoln)

2011
Andrew Johnson
Ulysses S. Grant
Rutherford B. Hayes
James A. Garfield

2012
Chester A. Arthur
Grover Cleveland
Benjamin Harrison
Grover Cleveland

2013
William McKinley
Theodore Roosevelt
William Howard Taft
Woodrow Wilson

2014
Warren Harding
Calvin Coolidge
Herbert Hoover
Franklin D. Roosevelt

2015
Harry S. Truman
Dwight D. Eisenhower
John F. Kennedy
Lyndon B. Johnson

2016
Richard M. Nixon
Gerald Ford

NATIVE AMERICAN DOLLARS (2009-)

The Native American $1 Coin Act, passed in 2007, mandated that the reverse of the Sacagawea dollar coin be changed each year beginning in 2009 to celebrate the contributions of Indian tribes and individual Native Americans to the country's development and history. The coins will be struck in addition to the Presidential Dollars. The law mandates that Native American Dollars make up at least 20 percent of the U.S. Mint's annual production of Native American and Presidential dollars combined.

The coins' obverses will continue to depict Sacagawea, the Native American woman who accompanied Lewis and Clark on their exploration of the American West. Like the Presidential Dollars, the date of issue, mintmark, and motto "E Pluribus Unum" appear as incused lettering on the edges of the Native American Dollars. The coins are struck in the same specifications as the Sacagawea coins, produced since 2000.

Uncirculated and proof versions of the Native American Dollars are also produced for sale to collectors.

The reverse of the inaugural coin in the series depicts a Native American woman planting seeds. The design is a tribute to the tradition and importance of agriculture in Native

American culture. The 2010 issue depicts the Hiawatha Belt, which symbolizes the five Native American nations that made up the Iroquois Confederacy. The central figure on the belt, a great white pine, symbolizes the Onondaga Nation. The four squares flanking it represent the Mohawk, Oneida, Cayuga, and Seneca nations.

The U.S. Mint said it would release a schedule of future design themes for the Native American Dollars going through at least the year 2016. The Mint said it would consult with the Senate Committee on Indian Affairs, House of Representatives Congressional Native American Caucus, National Congress of American Indians, U.S. Commission of Fine Arts, and the Citizens Coinage Advisory Committee in determining future designs. The U.S. Treasury secretary has final authority in the selection process.

Diameter: 26.4 millimeters. **Weight:** 8.07 grams. **Composition:** 88.5-percent copper, 6-percent zinc, 3.5-percent manganese, 2-percent nickel.

2009 Native American Dollar (obverse)

Agriculture

Date	Mintage	MS-63	MS-65	Proof-65
2009-P	37,380,000	2.50	6.00	—
2009-D	33,880,000	2.50	6.00	—
2009-S	—	—	—	22.50

2009 Native American Dollar (Agriculture)

Great Tree of Peace

Date	Mintage	MS-63	MS-65	Proof-65
2010-P	—	—	—	—
2010-D	—	—	—	—
2010-S	—	—	—	—

2010 Native American Dollar (Great Tree of Peace)

FIRST SPOUSE GOLD $10 COINS (2007-2016)

The Presidential $1 Coin Act of 2005 also authorized the minting of half-ounce gold $10 bullion coins honoring the wives of U.S. presidents. The women will be honored in the order in which they served, and the release schedule parallels the release schedule for the Presidential Dollars.

Obverse designs will include the name and likeness of the first spouse, the years during which her husband was president, and a number indicating the order in which her husband served. Reverse images will be emblematic of the spouse's life and work.

For presidents who were not married during their terms in office, the obverse design will include an image of Liberty as depicted on a U.S. coin that circulated during the president's term. Reverse designs will be based on "themes of such President" being honored.

An exception will be the coin for President Chester A. Arthur. The legislation mandates that the obverse depict Alice Paul, a leader in the women's suffrage movement. Paul was born Jan. 11, 1885, during Arthur's term. The reverse design will also represent the suffrage movement. The First Spouse coins contain a half-ounce of 24-karat gold (.9999 fine).

Diameter: 22 millimeters. Weight: 15.552 grams. **Composition:** 99.99-percent gold. **Actual gold weight:** .4999 troy ounces.

Martha Washington

Date	Mintage	MS-63	MS-65	Proof-65
2007-W	20,000	555.00	640.00	—
2007-W	20,000	—	—	640.00

2007-W First Spouse Gold $10 (Martha Washington)

Abigail Adams

Date	Mintage	MS-63	MS-65	Proof-65
2007-W	20,000	545.00	640.00	—
2007-W	20,000	—	—	640.00

2007-W First Spouse Gold $10 (Abigail Adams)

Thomas Jefferson

Date	Mintage	MS-63	MS-65	Proof-65
2007-W	20,000	555.00	640.00	—
2007-W	20,000	—	—	640.00

2007-W First Spouse Gold $10 (Thomas Jefferson)

Dolley Madison

Date	Mintage	MS-63	MS-65	Proof-65
2007-W	40,000	555.00	640.00	—
2007-W	Inc. above	—	—	640.00

2007-W First Spouse Gold $10 (Dolley Madison)

Elizabeth Monroe

Date	Mintage	MS-63	MS-65	Proof-65
2008-W	40,000	555.00	645.00	—
2008-W	Inc. above	—	—	645.00

2008-W First Spouse Gold $10 (Elizabeth Monroe)

Louisa Adams

Date	Mintage	MS-63	MS-65	Proof-65
2008-W	40,000	555.00	645.00	—
2008-W	Inc. above	—	—	645.00

2008-W First Spouse Gold $10 (Louisa Adams)

Andrew Jackson

Date	Mintage	MS-63	MS-65	Proof-65
2008-W	40,000	555.00	645.00	—
2008-W	Inc. above	—	—	645.00

2008-W First Spouse Gold $10 (Andrew Jackson)

Martin Van Buren

Date	Mintage	MS-63	MS-65	Proof-65
2008-W	40,000	555.00	645.00	—
2008-W	Inc. above	—	—	645.00

2008-W First Spouse Gold $10 (Martin Van Buren)

Anna Harrison

Date	Mintage	MS-63	MS-65	Proof-65
2009-W	40,000	625.00	650.00	—
2009-W	Inc. above	—	—	650.00

2009-W First Spouse Gold $10 (Anna Harrison)

Letitia Tyler

Date	Mintage	MS-63	MS-65	Proof-65
2009-W	40,000	—	625.00	—
2009-W	Inc. above	—	—	640.00

2009-W First Spouse Gold $10 (Letitia Tyler)

Julia Tyler

Date	Mintage	MS-63	MS-65	Proof-65
2009-W	40,000	—	625.00	—
2009-W	Inc. above	—	—	640.00

2009-W First Spouse Gold $10 (Julia Tyler)

Sarah Polk

Date	Mintage	MS-63	MS-65	Proof-65
2009-W	40,000	—	625.00	—
2009-W	Inc. above	—	—	640.00

2009-W First Spouse Gold $10 (Sarah Polk)

Margaret Taylor

Date	Mintage	MS-63	MS-65	Proof-65
2009-W	40,000	—	625.00	—
2009-W	Inc. above	—	—	640.00

2009-W First Spouse Gold $10 (Margaret Taylor)

Abigail Fillmore

Date	Mintage	MS-63	MS-65	Proof-65
2010-W	—	—	—	—
2010-W	—	—	—	—

2010-W First Spouse Gold $10 (Abigail Fillmore)

Jane Pierce				
Date	Mintage	MS-63	MS-65	Proof-65
2010-W	—	—	—	—
2010-W	—	—	—	—

2010-W First Spouse Gold $10 (Jane Pierce)

James Buchanan

Date	Mintage	MS-63	MS-65	Proof-65
2010-W	—	—	—	—
2010-W	—	—	—	—

2010-W First Spouse Gold $10 (James Buchanan)

Mary Todd Lincoln				
Date	Mintage	MS-63	MS-65	Proof-65
2010-W	—	—	—	—
2010-W	—	—	—	—

2010-W First Spouse Gold $10 (Mary Todd Lincoln)

2011
Eliza Johnson
Julia S. Grant
Lucy Hayes
Lucretia Garfield

2012
Alice Paul (Chester A. Arthur)
Frances Cleveland
Caroline Harrison
Frances Cleveland

2013
Ida McKinley
Edith Roosevelt
Helen Taft
Ellen Wilson, Edith Wilson

2014
Florence Harding
Grace Coolidge
Lou Hoover
Anna Eleanor Roosevelt

2015
Elizabeth Truman
Mamie Eisenhower
Jacqueline Kennedy
Claudia Taylor "Lady Bird" Johnson

2016
Patricia Ryan "Pat" Nixon

ULTRAHIGH-RELIEF GOLD $20 (2009)

The 2009 Ultrahigh-Relief Gold $20 revives what many consider to be the most beautiful design in U.S. coinage history.

Sculptor Augustus Saint-Gaudens designed President Theodore Roosevelt's inaugural medal. Roosevelt liked the medal so much he commissioned Saint-Gaudens to improve the design of U.S. coinage. Roosevelt wanted the gold $20 to emulate the high relief used on ancient Greek coins.

Saint-Gaudens designed a striking image of Liberty striding forward toward the viewer for the obverse and an eagle in flight for the reverse of the gold $20, or double eagle. Released in 1907, the coins were first produced in the high-relief style Roosevelt desired and used Roman numerals for the date. The motto "E Pluribus Unum" appeared as raised lettering on the coin's edge.

The high relief, however, caused production problems and would not allow the coins to stack properly. So later that year, the relief was lowered and the Roman numerals in the date were replaced by Arabic numerals. The Saint-Gaudens gold $20 was struck in this style through 1933, although most of the final year's mintage were never released into circulation and were eventually melted.

In early 2008, U.S. Mint Director Ed Moy announced his agency would again strike Saint-Gaudens gold $20 coins in the original high-relief style for sale to collectors. The Mint cited existing coinage law that grants the U.S. Treasury secretary certain authority to mint gold coins.

Technological advances today allowed the Mint to produce the coin in the ultrahigh relief Roosevelt envisioned. Mint staff digitally mapped the design working from Saint-Gaudens' original plaster models.

A few contemporary modifications were made to the 1907 design: The obverse of the new coin has 50 stars, representing the 50 states in the union, instead of the 46 stars on the original. The motto "In God We Trust" appears on the reverse of the new coin. The original 1907 version did not have the motto. Also, a small border was added to the new coin to create a "more consistent edge," according to the Mint.

True to the original, the new coin's date (2009) appears in Roman numerals and the motto "E Pluribus Unum" appears as raised lettering on the edge. The coins were produced at the West Point Mint but do not have a mintmark.

The new version was struck in 24-karat gold (.9999 fine). The original version was only 22 karats (.9000 fine). The U.S. Mint planned to produce the Ultrahigh-Relief Gold $20 for only one year with no mintage limit. Mint sales of the coin ended Dec. 31, 2009.

Diameter: 27 millimeters. **Weight:** 31.1 grams. **Composition:** 99.99-percent gold. **Actual gold weight:** 1 troy ounce.

Edge lettering on the 2009 Ultrahigh-Relief Gold $20.

Date	Mintage	Proof-65
2009	115,178	1,275.00

2009 Ultrahigh-Relief Gold $20

COMMEMORATIVES (1982-)

After a 28-year break, the U.S. Mint resumed issuing commemorative coins when it released a half dollar marking the 250th anniversary of George Washington's birth in 1982. The congressionally authorized coin was a hit. The Mint sold more than 2.2 million uncirculated versions and almost 4.9 million proof versions.

A myriad of issues have followed in clad, silver, and gold compositions, and in denominations ranging from a half dollar to $10.

Commemorative coins honor events, people, or other things, and are individually authorized by law. They are official U.S. government issues and legal tender, but they are not intended to circulate. Instead, the U.S. Mint sells the coins directly to collectors at a premium above face value. Laws authorizing commemorative coins usually mandate that a certain amount of the purchase price benefit a group or event related to the coin's theme.

By the 1990s, commemorative coins had become an easy mark for senators and U.S. representatives looking to do a favor for a constituency or a favor for a fellow lawmaker by offering their vote for a commemorative coin program. The year 1994 alone brought five commemorative coin programs, and the proliferation caused sales to plummet.

In response, Congress passed the Commemorative Coin Reform Act of 1996. Among other provisions, it limits the number of commemorative themes to two per year.

Current-year commemoratives can be purchased directly from the U.S. Mint (www.usmint.gov). Issues from previous years can be purchased on the secondary market (shows, shops, and advertisements in coin-collecting magazines) for the going market rate, as reflected in the values listed.

Clad Half Dollars

Diameter: 30.6 millimeters. **Weight:** 11.34 grams. **Composition:** clad layers of 75-percent copper and 25-percent nickel bonded to a pure-copper core.

Statue of Liberty Centennial			
Date	Mintage	MS-65	Proof-65
1986-D	928,008	5.25	—
1986-S	6,925,627	—	5.00

1986-S Commemorative Clad Half Dollar (Statue of Liberty Centennial)

Bicentennial of the Congress

Date	Mintage	MS-65	Proof-65
1989-D	163,753	7.50	—
1989-S	—	—	7.25

1989-D Commemorative Clad Half Dollar (Bicentennial of the Congress)

Mount Rushmore Golden Anniversary

Date	Mintage	MS-65	Proof-65
1991-D	172,754	19.50	—
1991-S	—	—	18.50

1991-S Commemorative Clad Half Dollar
(Mount Rushmore Golden Anniversary)

World War II 50th Anniversary (Issued in 1993.)			
Date	Mintage	MS-65	Proof-65
1991-1995-P	192,968	24.50	—
1991-1995-P	290,343	—	23.50

1991-1995-P Commemorative Clad Half Dollar
(World War II 50th Anniversary)

1992 Olympics

Date	Mintage	MS-65	Proof-65
1992-P	161,607	8.50	—
1992-S	519,645	—	9.00

1992-S Commemorative Clad Half Dollar (1992 Olympics)

500th Anniversary of Columbus Discovery

Date	Mintage	MS-65	Proof-65
1992-D	135,702	11.50	—
1992-S	390,154	—	10.50

*1992-S Commemorative Clad Half Dollar
(500th Anniversary of Columbus Discovery)*

1994 World Cup

Date	Mintage	MS-65	Proof-65
1994-D	168,208	9.00	—
1994-P	122,412	10.25	—
1994-P	609,354	—	8.00

1994-P Commemorative Clad Half Dollar (1994 World Cup)

1996 Atlanta Olympics (baseball design)

Date	Mintage	MS-65	Proof-65
1995-S	164,605	20.50	—
1995-S	118,087	—	18.00

1995-S Commemorative Clad Half Dollar
(1996 Atlanta Olympics – baseball design)

1996 Atlanta Olympics (basketball design)			
Date	Mintage	MS-65	Proof-65
1995-S	171,001	19.00	—
1995-S	169,655	—	16.00

1995-S Commemorative Clad Half Dollar
(1996 Atlanta Olympics – basketball design)

Civil War

Date	Mintage	MS-65	Proof-65
1995-S	119,510	39.50	—
1995-S	330,099	—	38.50

1995-S Commemorative Clad Half Dollar (Civil War)

1996 Atlanta Olympics (soccer design)

Date	Mintage	MS-65	Proof-65
1996-S	52,836	138.00	—
1996-S	122,412	—	100.00

1996-S Commemorative Clad Half Dollar
(1996 Atlanta Olympics – soccer design)

1996 Atlanta Olympics (swimming design)			
Date	Mintage	MS-65	Proof-65
1996-S	49,533	150.00	—
1996-S	114,315	—	34.50

1996-S Commemorative Clad Half Dollar
(1996 Atlanta Olympics – swimming design)

U.S. Capitol

Date	Mintage	MS-65	Proof-65
2001-P	99,157	13.50	—
2001-P	77,962	—	15.50

2001-P Commemorative Clad Half Dollar (U.S. Capitol)

First Flight Centennial

Date	Mintage	MS-65	Proof-65
2003-P	57,726	15.00	—
2003-P	111,569	—	16.00

2003-P Commemorative Clad Half Dollar (First Flight Centennial)

Bald Eagle

Date	Mintage	MS-65	Proof-65
2008-S	—	15.00	—
2008-S	—	—	20.00

2008-S Commemorative Clad Half Dollar (Bald Eagle)

Silver Half Dollars

Diameter: 38.1 millimeters. **Weight:** 26.73 grams. **Composition:** 90-percent silver, 10-percent copper. **Actual silver weight:** .76 troy ounces.

George Washington 250th Anniversary of Birth			
Date	Mintage	MS-65	Proof-65
1982-D	2,210,458	7.75	—
1982-S	4,894,044	—	7.75

1982-D Commemorative Silver Half Dollar
(George Washington 250th Anniversary of Birth)

James Madison, Bill of Rights

Date	Mintage	MS-65	Proof-65
1993-W	173,224	18.50	—
1993-S	559,758	—	15.00

1993-S Commemorative Silver Half Dollar (James Madison)

Silver Dollars

Diameter: 38.1 millimeters. **Weight:** 26.73 grams. **Composition:** 90-percent silver, 10-percent copper. **Actual silver weight:** .76 troy ounces.

Los Angeles XXIII Olympiad			
Date	Mintage	MS-65	Proof-65
1983-P	294,543	17.50	—
1983-D	174,014	18.50	—
1983-S	174,014	18.50	—
1983-S	1,577,025	—	18.00

1983-S Commemorative Silver Dollar (Los Angeles XXIII Olympiad)

Los Angeles XXIII Olympiad

Date	Mintage	MS-65	Proof-65
1984-P	217,954	17.50	—
1984-D	116,675	18.50	—
1984-S	116,675	18.50	—
1984-S	1,801,210	—	18.50

1984-S Commemorative Silver Dollar (Los Angeles XXIII Olympiad)

Statue of Liberty Centennial

Date	Mintage	MS-65	Proof-65
1986-P	723,635	18.00	—
1986-S	6,414,638	—	18.50

1986-S Commemorative Silver Dollar (Statue of Liberty Centennial)

The U.S. Constitution 200th Anniversary

Date	Mintage	MS-65	Proof-65
1987-P	451,629	18.00	—
1987-S	2,747,116	—	18.50

1987-S Commemorative Silver Dollar (The U.S. Constitution 200th Anniversary)

1988 Olympiad

Date	Mintage	MS-65	Proof-65
1988-D	191,368	18.00	—
1988-S	1,359,366	—	18.50

1988-S Commemorative Silver Dollar (1988 Olympiad)

Bicentennial of the Congress

Date	Mintage	MS-65	Proof-65
1989-D	135,203	21.50	—
1989-S	762,198	—	20.50

1989-D Commemorative Silver Dollar (Bicentennial of the Congress)

Eisenhower Centennial

Date	Mintage	MS-65	Proof-65
1990-W	241,669	18.00	—
1990-P	638,335	—	18.00

1990-P Commemorative Silver Dollar (Eisenhower Centennial)

38th Anniversary Korea

Date	Mintage	MS-65	Proof-65
1991-D	213,049	19.50	—
1991-P	618,488	—	20.00

1991-P Commemorative Silver Dollar (38th Anniversary Korea)

Mount Rushmore Golden Anniversary

Date	Mintage	MS-65	Proof-65
1991-P	133,139	28.50	—
1991-S	738,419	—	23.50

1991-S Commemorative Silver Dollar
(Mount Rushmore Golden Anniversary)

USO 50th Anniversary

Date	Mintage	MS-65	Proof-65
1991-D	124,958	18.00	—
1991-S	321,275	—	18.50

1991-S Commemorative Silver Dollar (USO 50th Anniversary)

World War II 50th Anniversary (Issued in 1993.)			
Date	Mintage	MS-65	Proof-65
1991-1995	94,708	29.50	—
1991-1995	322,422	—	37.50

1991-1995-W Commemorative Silver Dollar (World War II 50th Anniversary)

1992 Olympics

Date	Mintage	MS-65	Proof-65
1992-D	187,552	22.50	—
1992-S	504,505	—	24.50

1992-S Commemorative Silver Dollar (1992 Olympics)

Columbus Quincentenary			
Date	Mintage	MS-65	Proof-65
1992-D	106,949	26.00	—
1992-P	385,241	—	29.00

1992-P Commemorative Silver Dollar (Columbus Quincentenary)

The White House 1792-1992

Date	Mintage	MS-65	Proof-65
1992-D	123,803	26.00	—
1992-W	375,851	—	28.00

1992-W Commemorative Silver Dollar (The White House 1792-1992)

James Madison

Date	Mintage	MS-65	Proof-65
1993-D	98,383	18.50	—
1993-S	534,001	—	20.50

1993-S Commemorative Silver Dollar (James Madison)

Thomas Jefferson 1743-1993 (Issued in 1994.)			
Date	Mintage	MS-65	Proof-65
1993-P	266,927	18.50	—
1993-S	332,891	—	19.50

1993-P Commemorative Silver Dollar (Thomas Jefferson 1743-1993)

1994 World Cup

Date	Mintage	MS-65	Proof-65
1994-D	81,698	22.50	—
1994-S	576,978	—	23.50

1994-S Commemorative Silver Dollar (1994 World Cup)

National Prisoner of War Museum

Date	Mintage	MS-65	Proof-65
1994-W	54,790	85.00	—
1994-P	220,100	—	42.00

1994-P Commemorative Silver Dollar (National Prisoner of War Museum)

Bicentennial of United States Capitol

Date	Mintage	MS-65	Proof-65
1994-D	68,352	18.00	—
1994-S	279,416	—	22.50

1994-S Commemorative Silver Dollar (Bicentennial of United States Capitol)

Vietnam Veterans Memorial

Date	Mintage	MS-65	Proof-65
1994-W	57,317	80.00	—
1994-P	226,262	—	65.00

1994-P Commemorative Silver Dollar (Vietnam Veterans Memorial)

Women in Military Service Memorial

Date	Mintage	MS-65	Proof-65
1994-W	53,054	36.50	—
1994-P	213,201	—	30.00

1994-P Commemorative Silver Dollar
(Women in Military Service Memorial)

1996 Atlanta Olympics (cycling design)			
Date	Mintage	MS-65	Proof-65
1995-D	19,662	142.00	—
1995-P	118,795	—	46.00

1995-P Commemorative Silver Dollar
(1996 Atlanta Olympics – cycling design)

1996 Atlanta Olympics (gymnastics design)

Date	Mintage	MS-65	Proof-65
1995-D	42,497	67.50	—
1995-P	182,676	—	50.00

1995-P Commemorative Silver Dollar
(1996 Atlanta Olympics – gymnastics design)

1996 Atlanta Olympics (track and field design)			
Date	Mintage	MS-65	Proof-65
1995-D	24,796	92.00	—
1995-P	136,935	—	49.00

1995-P Commemorative Silver Dollar
(1996 Atlanta Olympics – track and field design)

1996 Atlanta Olympics (Paralympics design)

Date	Mintage	MS-65	Proof-65
1995-D	28,649	82.00	—
1995-P	138,337	—	54.00

1995-P Commemorative Silver Dollar
(1996 Atlanta Olympics – Paralympics design)

Civil War			
Date	Mintage	MS-65	Proof-65
1995-P	45,866	70.00	—
1995-S	437,114	—	70.00

1995-S Commemorative Silver Dollar (Civil War)

Special Olympics World Games

Date	Mintage	MS-65	Proof-65
1995-W	89,301	29.50	—
1995-P	351,764	—	26.50

1995-P Commemorative Silver Dollar (Special Olympics World Games)

1996 Atlanta Olympics (high-jump design)			
Date	Mintage	MS-65	Proof-65
1996-D	15,697	380.00	—
1996-P	124,502	—	58.00

1996-P Commemorative Silver Dollar
(1996 Atlanta Olympics – high-jump design)

1996 Atlanta Olympics (rowing design)			
Date	Mintage	MS-65	Proof-65
1996-D	16,258	345.00	—
1996-P	151,890	—	70.00

1996-P Commemorative Silver Dollar
(1996 Atlanta Olympics – rowing design)

1996 Atlanta Olympics (tennis design)			
Date	Mintage	MS-65	Proof-65
1996-D	15,983	315.00	—
1996-P	92,016	—	85.00

1996-P Commemorative Silver Dollar
(1996 Atlanta Olympics – tennis design)

1996 Atlanta Olympics (Paralympics design)			
Date	Mintage	MS-65	Proof-65
1996-D	14,497	365.00	—
1996-P	84,280	—	82.00

1996-P Commemorative Silver Dollar
(1996 Atlanta Olympics – Paralympics design)

National Community Service

Date	Mintage	MS-65	Proof-65
1996-S	23,500	220.00	—
1996-S	101,543	—	76.00

1996-S Commemorative Silver Dollar (National Community Service)

Smithsonian Institution 1846-1996

Date	Mintage	MS-65	Proof-65
1996-D	31,230	135.00	—
1996-P	129,152	—	57.50

1996-P Commemorative Silver Dollar (Smithsonian Institution 1846-1996)

Jackie Robinson 50th Anniversary

Date	Mintage	MS-65	Proof-65
1997-S	30,007	98.00	—
1997-S	110,495	—	118.00

1997-S Commemorative Silver Dollar (Jackie Robinson 50th Anniversary)

National Law Enforcement Officers Memorial

Date	Mintage	MS-65	Proof-65
1997-P	28,575	160.00	—
1997-P	110,428	—	105.00

1997-P Commemorative Silver Dollar
(National Law Enforcement Officers Memorial)

United States Botanic Garden 1820-1995

Date	Mintage	MS-65	Proof-65
1997-P	57,272	40.00	—
1997-P	264,528	38.00	—

1997-P Commemorative Silver Dollar
(United States Botanic Garden 1820-1995)

Black Revolutionary War Patriots

Date	Mintage	MS-65	Proof-65
1998-S	37,210	160.00	—
1998-S	75,070	—	96.00

1998-S Commemorative Silver Dollar (Black Revolutionary War Patriots)

Robert F. Kennedy

Date	Mintage	MS-65	Proof-65
1998-S	106,422	31.50	—
1998-S	99,020	—	42.50

1998-S Commemorative Silver Dollar (Robert F. Kennedy)

Dolley Madison

Date	Mintage	MS-65	Proof-65
1999-P	22,948	42.00	—
1999-P	158,247	—	34.50

1999-P Commemorative Silver Dollar (Dolley Madison)

Yellowstone National Park

Date	Mintage	MS-65	Proof-65
1999-P	23,614	50.00	—
1999-P	128,646	—	45.00

1999-P Commemorative Silver Dollar (Yellowstone National Park)

Leif Ericson

Date	Mintage	MS-65	Proof-65
2000-P	28,150	87.00	—
2000-P	58,612	—	70.00

2000-P Commemorative Silver Dollar (Leif Ericson)

Library of Congress 1800-2000

Date	Mintage	MS-65	Proof-65
2000-P	52,771	38.00	—
2000-P	196,900	—	33.00

2000-P Commemorative Silver Dollar (Library of Congress 1800-2000)

American Buffalo

Date	Mintage	MS-65	Proof-65
2001-D	197,131	175.00	—
2001-P	272,869	—	180.00

2001-D Commemorative Silver Dollar (American Buffalo)

U.S. Capitol

Date	Mintage	MS-65	Proof-65
2001-P	66,636	30.00	—
2001-P	143,793	—	39.00

2001-P Commemorative Silver Dollar (U.S. Capitol)

XIX Olympic Winter Games

Date	Mintage	MS-65	Proof-65
2002-P	35,388	30.00	—
2002-P	142,873	—	38.00

2002-P Commemorative Silver Dollar (XIX Olympic Winter Games)

West Point Bicentennial

Date	Mintage	MS-65	Proof-65
2002-W	103,201	18.50	—
2002-W	288,293	—	18.50

2002-W Commemorative Silver Dollar (West Point Bicentennial)

First Flight Centennial

Date	Mintage	MS-65	Proof-65
2003-P	53,761	33.50	—
2003-P	193,086	—	28.50

2003-P Commemorative Silver Dollar (First Flight Centennial)

Lewis and Clark Bicentennial

Date	Mintage	MS-65	Proof-65
2004-P	90,323	31.00	—
2004-P	288,492	—	27.50

2004-P Commemorative Silver Dollar (Lewis and Clark Bicentennial)

125th Anniversary of the Light Bulb

Date	Mintage	MS-65	Proof-65
2004-P	68,031	34.00	—
2004-P	213,409	—	34.50

2004-P Commemorative Silver Dollar (125th Anniversary of the Light Bulb)

Chief Justice John Marshall

Date	Mintage	MS-65	Proof-65
2005-P	67,096	32.00	—
2005-P	196,753	—	35.00

2005-P Commemorative Silver Dollar (Chief Justice John Marshall)

Marines 1775-2005

Date	Mintage	MS-65	Proof-65
2005-P	130,000	37.00	—
2005-P	370,000	—	39.00

2005-P Commemorative Silver Dollar (Marines 1775-2005)

Benjamin Franklin Tercentenary (kite-flying design)

Date	Mintage	MS-65	Proof-65
2006-P	58,000	32.00	—
2006-P	142,000	—	45.00

2006-P Commemorative Silver Dollar
(Benjamin Franklin Tercentenary – kite-flying design)

Benjamin Franklin Tercentenary (portrait design)

Date	Mintage	MS-65	Proof-65
2006-P	58,000	33.00	—
2006-P	142,000	—	44.00

2006-P Commemorative Silver Dollar
(Benjamin Franklin Tercentenary – portrait design)

San Francisco Old Mint

Date	Mintage	MS-65	Proof-65
2006-S	67,100	41.00	—
2006-S	160,870	—	42.00

2006-S Commemorative Silver Dollar (San Francisco Old Mint)

Desegregation in Education

Date	Mintage	MS-65	Proof-65
2007-P	—	50.00	—
2007-P	—	—	50.00

2007-P Commemorative Silver Dollar (Desegregation in Education)

Founding of Jamestown 1607-2007

Date	Mintage	MS-65	Proof-65
2007-P	—	36.50	—
2007-P	—	—	35.00

2007-P Commemorative Silver Dollar (Founding of Jamestown 1607-2007)

Bald Eagle

Date	Mintage	MS-65	Proof-65
2008-P	119,204	40.00	—
2008-P	294,601	—	38.50

2008-P Commemorative Silver Dollar (Bald Eagle)

Abraham Lincoln

Date	Mintage	MS-65	Proof-65
2009-P	—	41.00	—
2009-P	—	—	38.50

2009-P Commemorative Silver Dollar (Abraham Lincoln)

Louis Braille 1809-2009

Date	Mintage	MS-65	Proof-65
2009-P	—	32.50	—
2009-P	—	—	42.50

2009-P Commemorative Silver Dollar (Louis Braille 1809-2009)

Disabled Veterans

Date	Mintage	MS-65	Proof-65
2010-W	—	—	—
2010-W	—	—	—

2010-W Commemorative Silver Dollar (Disabled Veterans)

Boy Scouts of America 1910-2010

Date	Mintage	MS-65	Proof-65
2010-P	—	—	—
2010-P	—	—	—

2010-P Commemorative Silver Dollar (Boy Scouts of America 1910-2010)

Medal of Honor	2011
U.S. Infantry	2012
Girl Scouts of America	2013

Gold $5

Diameter: 21.5 millimeters. **Weight:** 8.359 grams. **Composition:** 90-percent gold, 10-percent alloy. **Actual silver weight:** .24 troy ounces.

Statue of Liberty Centennial			
Date	Mintage	MS-65	Proof-65
1986-W	95,248	330.00	—
1986-W	404,013	—	330.00

1986-W Commemorative Gold $5 (Statue of Liberty Centennial)
Photos courtesy of Heritage Auction Galleries.

Bicentennial of the Constitution

Date	Mintage	MS-65	Proof-65
1987-W	214,225	330.00	—
1987-W	651,659	—	330.00

1987-W Commemorative Gold $5 (Bicentennial of the Constitution)
Photos courtesy of Heritage Auction Galleries.

1988 Olympiad

Date	Mintage	MS-65	Proof-65
1988-W	62,913	330.00	—
1988-W	281,456	—	330.00

1988-W Proof Commemorative Gold $5 (1988 Olympiad)
Photos courtesy of Heritage Auction Galleries.

Bicentennial of the Congress

Date	Mintage	MS-65	Proof-65
1989-W	46,899	330.00	—
1989-W	164,690	—	330.00

1989-W Commemorative Gold $5 (Bicentennial of the Congress)

Mount Rushmore National Memorial

Date	Mintage	MS-65	Proof-65
1991-W	31,959	395.00	—
1991-W	111,991	—	345.00

1991-W Commemorative Gold $5 (Mount Rushmore National Memorial)

World War II 50th Anniversary (Issued in 1993.)

Date	Mintage	MS-65	Proof-65
1991-1995-W	23,080	465.00	—
1991-1995-W	65,461	—	385.00

1991-1995-W Commemorative Gold $5 (World War II 50th Anniversary)

1992 Olympics

Date	Mintage	MS-65	Proof-65
1992-W	27,732	395.00	—
1992-W	77,313	—	345.00

1992-W Commemorative Gold $5 (1992 Olympics)

Columbus Quincentenary

Date	Mintage	MS-65	Proof-65
1992-W	24,329	395.00	—
1992-W	79,730	—	345.00

1992-W Commemorative Gold $5 (Columbus Quincentenary)

James Madison

Date	Mintage	MS-65	Proof-65
1993-W	22,266	435.00	—
1993-W	78,651	—	345.00

1993-W Commemorative Gold $5 (James Madison)

1994 World Cup

Date	Mintage	MS-65	Proof-65
1994-W	22,464	375.00	—
1994-W	89,619	—	385.00

1994-W Commemorative Gold $5 (1994 World Cup)
Photos courtesy of Heritage Auction Galleries.

1996 Atlanta Olympics (stadium design)

Date	Mintage	MS-65	Proof-65
1995-W	10,579	2,400.00	—
1995-W	43,124	—	575.00

1995-W Commemorative Gold $5 (1996 Atlanta Olympics – stadium design)
Photos courtesy of Heritage Auction Galleries.

1996 Atlanta Olympics (torch-runner design)

Date	Mintage	MS-65	Proof-65
1995-W	14,675	900.00	—
1995-W	57,442	—	375.00

1995-W Commemorative Gold $5 (1996 Atlanta Olympics – torch-runner design)
Photos courtesy of Heritage Auction Galleries.

Civil War

Date	Mintage	MS-65	Proof-65
1995-W	12,735	925.00	—
1995-W	55,246	—	395.00

1995-W Commemorative Gold $5 (Civil War)

1996 Atlanta Olympics (cauldron design)

Date	Mintage	MS-65	Proof-65
1996-W	9,210	2,650.00	—
1996-W	38,555	—	575.00

1996-W Commemorative Gold $5 (1996 Atlanta Olympics – cauldron design)
Photos courtesy of Heritage Auction Galleries.

1996 Atlanta Olympics (flag-bearer design)			
Date	Mintage	MS-65	Proof-65
1996-W	9,174	2,650.00	—
1996-W	32,886	—	635.00

1996-W Commemorative Gold $5 (1996 Atlanta Olympics – flag-bearer design)
Photos courtesy of Heritage Auction Galleries.

Smithsonian Institution 1846-1996

Date	Mintage	MS-65	Proof-65
1996-W	9,068	900.00	—
1996-W	29,474	—	495.00

1996-W Commemorative Gold $5 (Smithsonian Institution 1846-1996)

Franklin Delano Roosevelt

Date	Mintage	MS-65	Proof-65
1997-W	11,894	1,600.00	—
1997-W	29,474	—	400.00

1997-W Commemorative Gold $5 (Franklin Delano Roosevelt)

Jackie Robinson 50th Anniversary

Date	Mintage	MS-65	Proof-65
1997-W	5,202	3,900.00	—
1997-W	24,546	—	575.00

1997-W Commemorative Gold $5 (Jackie Robinson 50th Anniversary)
Photos courtesy of Heritage Auction Galleries.

George Washington (Bicentennial of Death)

Date	Mintage	MS-65	Proof-65
1999-W	22,511	400.00	—
1999-W	41,693	—	375.00

1999-W Commemorative Gold $5 (George Washington Bicentennial of Death)

U.S. Capitol

Date	Mintage	MS-65	Proof-65
2001-W	6,761	1,750.00	—
2001-W	27,652	—	420.00

2001-W Commemorative Gold $5 (U.S. Capitol)
Photos courtesy of Heritage Auction Galleries.

XIX Olympic Winter Games

Date	Mintage	MS-65	Proof-65
2002-W	10,585	440.00	—
2002-W	32,877	—	365.00

2002-W Commemorative Gold $5 (XIX Olympic Winter Games)

San Francisco Old Mint			
Date	Mintage	MS-65	Proof-65
2006-S	17,500	285.00	—
2006-S	44,174	—	300.00

2006-S Commemorative Gold $5 (San Francisco Old Mint)

Founding of Jamestown 1607-2007

Date	Mintage	MS-65	Proof-65
2007-W	—	345.00	—
2007-W	—	—	345.00

2007-W Commemorative Gold $5 (Founding of Jamestown 1607-2007)

Bald Eagle

Date	Mintage	MS-65	Proof-65
2008-W	—	285.00	—
2008-W	—	—	300.00

2008-W Commemorative Gold $5 (Bald Eagle)

Medal of Honor   2011

Gold $10

Diameter: 27 millimeters. **Weight:** 26.73 grams. **Composition:** 90-percent gold, 10-percent alloy. **Actual silver weight:** .484 troy ounces.

Los Angeles XXIII Olympiad			
Date	Mintage	MS-65	Proof-65
1984-W	75,886	610.00	—
1984-P	33,309	—	650.00
1984-D	34,533	—	650.00
1984-S	48,551	—	650.00
1984-W	381,085	—	650.00

1984-W Commemorative Gold $10 (Los Angeles XXIII Olympiad)

Weight: 16.259 grams. **Composition:** 48-percent platinum, 48-percent gold, 4-percent alloy.

Library of Congress 1800-2000			
Date	Mintage	MS-65	Proof-65
2000-W	6,683	5,950.00	—
2000-W	27,167	—	1,075.00

2000-W Commemorative Gold $10 (Library of Congress)

First Flight Centennial			
Date	Mintage	MS-65	Proof-65
2003-P	10,129	650.00	—
2003-P	21,846	—	650.00

2003-P Commemorative Gold $10 (First Flight Centennial)

COMMEMORATIVE SETS (1983-)

The U.S. Mint has packaged current-year commemorative coins in various combinations and offered them as sets. In some cases, commemorative coins have been packaged with uncirculated and proof versions of circulating coins related to the commemorative's theme or even non-numismatic items related to the commemorative's theme.

Prestige Sets package one or more commemorative coins with that year's proof versions of circulating coins. See the Proof Sets section for listings.

Current-year sets can be purchased directly from the U.S. Mint (www.usmint.gov). Sets from previous years can be purchased on the secondary market at the going price. Values listed below are for officially issued U.S. Mint sets in their original packaging.

Los Angeles XXIII Olympiad Sets	Value
(1) 1983-P uncirculated silver dollar, (2) 1984-P uncirculated silver dollar, (3) 1984-W uncirculated gold $10	455.00
(1) 1983-S proof silver dollar, (2) 1984-S proof silver dollar, (3) 1984-W proof gold $10	455.00

Los Angeles XXIII Olympiad Sets	Value
(1) 1983-S uncirculated silver dollar, (2) 1983-S proof silver dollar, (3) 1984-S uncirculated silver dollar, (4) 1984-S proof silver dollar, (5) 1984-W uncirculated gold $10, (6) 1984-W proof gold $10	910.00
(1) 1983-S proof silver dollar, (2) 1984-S proof silver dollar	22.50
(1) 1983-P uncirculated silver dollar, (2) 1983-D uncirculated silver dollar, (3) 1983-S uncirculated silver dollar	37.50
(1) 1984-P uncirculated silver dollar, (2) 1984-D uncirculated silver dollar, (3) 1984-S uncirculated silver dollar	38.50

1983 (P, W, and S) Commemorative Set,
Los Angeles XXIII Olympiad (obverses)

1984 (P, W, and S) Commemorative Set, Los Angeles XXIII Olympiad (obverses)

Statue of Liberty Centennial Sets	Value
(1) 1986-D uncirculated clad half dollar, (2) 1986-P uncirculated silver dollar	17.00
(1) 1986-S proof clad half dollar, (2) 1986-S proof silver dollar	17.00
(1) 1986-D uncirculated clad half dollar, (2) 1986-P uncirculated silver dollar, (3) 1986-W uncirculated gold $10	225.00
(1) 1986-S proof clad half dollar, (2) 1986-S proof silver dollar, (3) 1986-W proof gold $5	225.00
(1) 1986-D uncirculated clad half dollar, (2) 1986-S proof clad half dollar, (3) 1986-P uncirculated silver dollar, (4) 1986-S proof silver dollar, (5) 1986-W uncirculated gold $5, (6) 1986-W proof gold $5	450.00

The U.S. Constitution 200th Anniversary Sets	Value
(1) 1987-P uncirculated silver dollar, (2) 1987-W uncirculated gold $5	220.00
(1) 1987-S proof silver dollar, (2) 1987-W proof gold $5	220.00
(1) 1987-P uncirculated silver dollar, (2) 1987-S proof silver dollar, (3-4) 1987-W uncirculated and proof gold $5	445.00

1988 Olympiad Sets	Value
(1) 1988-D uncirculated silver dollar, (2) 1988-W uncirculated gold $5	220.00
(1) 1988-S proof silver dollar, (2) 1988-W proof gold $5	220.00
(1) 1988-D uncirculated silver dollar, (2) 1988-S proof silver dollar, (3-4) 1988-W uncirculated and proof gold $5	440.00

Bicentennial of the Congress Sets	Value
(1) 1989-D uncirculated clad half dollar, (2) 1989-D uncirculated silver dollar	20.00
(1) 1989-S proof clad half dollar, (2) 1989-S proof silver dollar	21.00
(1) 1989-D uncirculated clad half dollar, (2) 1989-D uncirculated silver dollar, (3) 1989-W uncirculated gold $5	220.00
(1) 1989-S proof clad half dollar, (2) 1989-S proof silver dollar, (3) 1989-W proof gold $5	220.00
(1) 1989-D uncirculated clad half dollar, (2) 1989-S proof clad half dollar, (3) 1989-D uncirculated silver dollar, (4) 1989-S proof silver dollar, (5-6) 1989-W uncirculated and proof gold $5	440.00

Mount Rushmore Golden Anniversary Sets	Value
(1) 1991-D uncirculated clad half dollar, (2) 1991-P uncirculated silver dollar	45.00
(1) 1991-S proof clad half dollar, (2) 1991-S proof silver dollar	45.00
(1) 1991-D uncirculated clad half dollar, (2) 1991-P uncirculated silver dollar, (3) 1991-W uncirculated gold $5	300.00
(1) 1991-S proof clad half dollar, (2) 1991-S proof silver dollar, (3) 1991-W proof gold $5	225.00
(1) 1991-D uncirculated clad half dollar, (2) 1991-S proof clad half dollar, (3) 1991-P uncirculated silver dollar, (4) 1991-S proof silver dollar, (5-6) 1991-W uncirculated and proof gold $5	495.00

World War II 50th Anniversary Sets (Issued in 1993.)	Value
(1) 1991-1995-P uncirculated clad half dollar, (2) 1991-1995-D uncirculated silver dollar	49.00
(1) 1991-1995-P proof clad half dollar, (2) 1991-1995-W proof silver dollar	55.00
(1) 1991-1995-P uncirculated clad half dollar, (2) 1991-1995-D uncirculated silver dollar, (3) 1991-1995-W uncirculated gold $5	345.00
(1) 1991-1995-P proof clad half dollar, (2) 1991-1995-W proof silver dollar, (3) 1991-1995-W proof gold $5	335.00
(1-2) 1991-1995-P uncirculated and proof clad half dollars, (3) 1991-1995-D uncirculated silver dollar, (4) 1991-1995-W proof silver dollar, (5-6) 1991-1995-W uncirculated and proof gold $5	665.00

1992 Olympics Sets	Value
(1) 1992-P uncirculated clad half dollar, (2) 1992-D uncirculated silver dollar	28.00
(1) 1992-S proof clad half dollar, (2) 1992-S proof silver dollar	28.00
(1) 1992-P uncirculated clad half dollar, (2) 1992-D uncirculated silver dollar, (3) 1992-W uncirculated gold $5	275.00
(1) 1992-S proof clad half dollar, (2) 1992-S proof silver dollar, (3) 1992-W proof gold $5	240.00
(1) 1992-P uncirculated clad half dollar, (2) 1992-S proof clad half dollar, (3) 1992-D uncirculated silver dollar, (4) 1992-S proof silver dollar, (5-6) 1992-W uncirculated and proof gold $5	520.00

Columbus Quincentenary Sets	Value
(1) 1992-D uncirculated clad half dollar, (2) 1992-D uncirculated silver dollar	35.00
(1) 1992-S proof clad half dollar, (2) 1992-P proof silver dollar	39.00
(1) 1992-D uncirculated clad half dollar, (2) 1992-D uncirculated silver dollar, (3) 1992-W uncirculated gold $5	320.00
(1) 1992-S proof clad half dollar, (2) 1992-P proof silver dollar, (3) 1992-W proof gold $5	265.00
(1) 1992-D uncirculated clad half dollar, (2) 1992-S proof clad half dollar, (3) 1992-D uncirculated silver dollar, (4) 1992-P proof silver dollar, (5-6) 1992-W uncirculated and proof gold $5	780.00

Thomas Jefferson 1743-1993 Sets (Issued in 1994.)	Value
(1) 1993-P uncirculated silver dollar, (2) 1994-P matte proof Jefferson nickel, (3) $2 Federal Reserve note	100.00

James Madison Sets	Value
(1) 1993-W uncirculated silver half dollar, (2) 1993-D uncirculated silver dollar	28.00
(1) 1993-S proof silver half dollar, (2) 1993-S proof silver dollar	29.00
(1) 1993-W uncirculated silver half dollar, (2) 1993-D uncirculated silver dollar, (3) 1993-W uncirculated gold $5	320.00
(1) 1993-S proof silver half dollar, (2) 1993-S proof silver dollar, (3) 1993-W proof gold $5	250.00
(1) 1993-W uncirculated silver half dollar, (2) 1993-S proof silver half dollar, (3) 1993-D uncirculated silver dollar, (4) 1993-S proof silver dollar, (5-6) 1993-W uncirculated and proof gold $5	550.00

1994 World Cup Sets	Value
(1) 1994-D uncirculated clad half dollar, (2) 1994-D uncirculated silver dollar	32.00
(1) 1994-P proof clad half dollar, (2) 1994-S proof silver dollar	37.00
(1) 1994-D uncirculated clad half dollar, (2) 1994-D uncirculated silver dollar, (3) 1994-W uncirculated gold $5	290.00
(1) 1994-P proof clad half dollar, (2) 1994-S proof silver dollar, (3) 1994-W proof gold $5	250.00

1994 World Cup Sets	Value
(1) 1994-D uncirculated clad half dollar, (2) 1994-P proof clad half dollar, (3) 1994-D uncirculated silver dollar, (4) 1994-S proof silver dollar, (5-6) 1994-W uncirculated and proof gold $5	525.00

U.S. Veterans Sets	Value
(1) 1994-W uncirculated National Prisoner of War silver dollar, (2) 1994-W uncirculated Vietnam Veterans Memorial silver dollar, (3) 1994-W uncirculated Women in Military Service Memorial silver dollar	170.00
(1) 1994-P proof National Prisoner of War silver dollar, (2) 1994-P proof Vietnam Veterans Memorial silver dollar, (3) 1994-P proof Women in Military Service Memorial silver dollar	120.00

1996 Atlanta Olympics Sets	Value
(1) 1995-S uncirculated clad half dollar basketball design, (2) 1995-D uncirculated silver dollar gymnastics design, (3) 1995-D uncirculated silver dollar Paralympics design, (4) 1995-W uncirculated gold $5 torch-runner design	715.00
(1) 1995-S proof clad half dollar basketball design, (2) 1995-P proof silver dollar gymnastics design, (3) 1995-P proof silver dollar Paralympics design, (4) 1995-W proof gold $5 torch-runner design	415.00
(1) 1995-P proof silver dollar gymnastics design, (2) 1995-P proof silver dollar Paralympics design	105.00

1996 Atlanta Olympics Sets	Value
(1) 1995-P proof silver dollar cycling design, (2) 1995-P proof silver dollar track and field design	95.00
(1) 1995-S proof clad half dollar basketball design, (2) 1995-S proof clad half dollar baseball design, (3) 1996-S proof clad half dollar soccer design, (4) 1996-S proof clad half dollar swimming design	140.00
(1) 1995-P proof silver dollar gymnastics design, (2) 1995-P proof silver dollar track and field design, (3) 1995-P proof silver dollar cycling design, (4) 1995-P proof silver dollar Paralympics design, (5) 1996-P proof silver dollar tennis design, (6) 1996-P proof silver dollar rowing design, (7) 1996-P proof silver dollar high-jump design, (8) 1996-P proof silver dollar Paralympics design	2,150.00
(1) 1995-D uncirculated silver dollar gymnastics design (2) 1995-P proof silver dollar gymnastics design (3) 1995-D uncirculated silver dollar track and field design (4) 1995-P proof silver dollar track and field design (5) 1995-D uncirculated silver dollar cycling design (6) 1995-P proof silver dollar cycling design (7) 1995-D uncirculated silver dollar Paralympics design (8) 1995-P proof silver dollar Paralympics design (9) 1996-D uncirculated silver dollar tennis design (10) 1996-P proof silver dollar tennis design (11) 1996-D uncirculated silver dollar rowing design (12) 1996-P proof silver dollar rowing design (13) 1996-D uncirculated silver dollar high-jump design (14) 1996-P proof silver dollar high-jump design (15) 1996-D uncirculated silver dollar Paralympics design (16) 1996-P proof silver dollar Paralympics design	2,350.00

1996 Atlanta Olympics Sets	Value
(1) 1995-S proof clad half dollar basketball design	2,400.00
(2) 1995-S proof clad half dollar baseball design	
(3) 1996-S proof clad half dollar soccer design	
(4) 1996-S proof clad half dollar swimming design	
(5) 1995-P proof silver dollar gymnastics design	
(6) 1995-P proof silver dollar track and field design	
(7) 1995-P proof silver dollar cycling design	
(8) 1995-P proof silver dollar Paralympics design	
(9) 1996-P proof silver dollar tennis design	
(10) 1996-P proof silver dollar rowing design	
(11) 1996-P proof silver dollar high-jump design	
(12) 1996-P proof silver dollar Paralympics design	
(13) 1995-W proof gold $5 torch-runner design	
(14) 1995-W proof gold $5 stadium design	
(15) 1996-W proof gold $5 cauldron design	
(16) 1996-W proof gold $5 flag-bearer design	

1996 Atlanta Olympics Sets	Value
(1-2) 1995-S uncirculated and proof clad half dollars basketball design, (3-4) 1995-S uncirculated and proof clad half dollars baseball design, (5-6) 1996-S uncirculated and proof clad half dollars soccer design, (7-8) 1996-S uncirculated and proof clad half dollars swimming design, (9) 1995-D uncirculated silver dollar gymnastics design, (10) 1995-P proof silver dollar gymnastics design, (11) 1995-D uncirculated silver dollar track and field design, (12) 1995-P proof silver dollar track and field design, (13) 1995-D uncirculated silver dollar cycling design, (14) 1995-P proof silver dollar cycling design, (15) 1995-D uncirculated silver dollar Paralympics design, (16) 1995-P proof silver dollar Paralympics design, (17) 1996-D uncirculated silver dollar tennis design, (18) 1996-P proof silver dollar tennis design, (19) 1996-D uncirculated silver dollar rowing design, (20) 1996-P proof silver dollar rowing design, (21) 1996-D uncirculated silver dollar high-jump design, (22) 1996-P proof silver dollar high-jump design, (23) 1996-D uncirculated silver dollar Paralympics design, (24) 1996-P proof silver dollar Paralympics design, (25-26) 1995-W uncirculated and proof gold $5 torch-runner design, (27-28) 1995-W uncirculated and proof gold $5 stadium design, (29-30) 1996-W uncirculated and proof gold $5 cauldron design, (31-32) 1996-W uncirculated and proof gold $5 flag-bearer design	6,600.00
(1) 1996-P proof silver dollar tennis design, (2) 1996-P proof silver dollar Paralympics design	160.00
(1) 1996-P proof silver dollar rowing design, (2) 1996-P proof silver dollar high-jump design	130.00

Civil War Sets	Value
(1) 1995-S uncirculated clad half dollar, (2) 1995-P uncirculated silver dollar	90.00
(1) 1995-S proof clad half dollar, (2) 1995-S proof silver dollar	100.00
(1) 1995-S uncirculated clad half dollar, (2) 1995-P uncirculated silver dollar, (3) 1995-W uncirculated gold $5	800.00
(1) 1995-S proof clad half dollar, (2) 1995-S proof silver dollar, (3) 1995-W proof gold $5	500.00
(1) 1995-S uncirculated clad half dollar, (2) 1995-S proof clad half dollar, (3) 1995-P uncirculated silver dollar, (4) 1995-S proof silver dollar, (5) 1995-W uncirculated gold $5, (6) 1995-W proof gold $5	1,275.00
Smithsonian Institution 1846-1996 Sets	**Value**
(1) 1996-P proof silver dollar, (2) 1996-W proof gold $5	615.00
(1) 1996-D uncirculated silver dollar, (2) 1996-P proof silver dollar, (3-4) 1996-W uncirculated and proof gold $5	2,100.00
Jackie Robinson 50th Anniversary Sets	**Value**
(1) 1997-S proof silver dollar, (2) 1997-W proof gold $5	800.00
(1-2) 1997-S uncirculated and proof silver dollars, (3-4) 1997-W uncirculated and proof gold $5	5,750.00
(1) 1997-W proof gold $5, (2) 1952 Topps Jackie Robinson baseball-card reproduction, (3) commemorative lapel pin	850.00

United States Botanic Garden 1820-1995 Set	Value
(1) 1997-P uncirculated silver dollar, (2) 1997-P uncirculated matte Jefferson nickel, (3) $1 Federal Reserve note	230.00

Franklin Delano Roosevelt Set	Value
(1-2) 1997-W uncirculated and proof gold $5	1,350.00

Robert F. Kennedy Sets	Value
(1) 1998-S uncirculated silver dollar, (2) 1998-S proof silver dollar	70.00
(1) 1998-S uncirculated silver dollar, (2) 1998-S matte proof John Kennedy half dollar	325.00

Black Revolutionary War Patriots Set	Value
(1-2) 1998-S uncirculated and proof silver dollars	200.00

George Washington (bicentennial of death) Set	Value
(1-2) 1999-W uncirculated and proof gold $5	800.00

Dolley Madison Set	Value
(1-2) 1999-P uncirculated and proof silver dollars	77.00

Yellowstone National Park Set	Value
(1-2) 1999-P uncirculated and proof silver dollars	88.00

Leif Ericson Set	Value
(1-2) 2000-P uncirculated and proof silver dollars	84.00

U.S. Capitol Set	Value
(1) 2001-P proof clad half dollar, (2) 2001-P proof silver dollar, (3) 2001-W proof gold $5	445.00

American Buffalo Set	Value
(1-2) 1997-W uncirculated and proof gold $5	1,350.00

Robert F. Kennedy Sets	Value
(1) 2001-D uncirculated silver dollar, (2) 2001-P proof silver dollar	460.00
(1) 2001-D uncirculated silver dollar, (2) 1899 $5 silver certificate replica	240.00

XIX Olympic Winter Games Sets	Value
(1) 2002-P proof silver dollar, (2) 2002-W proof gold $5	84.00
(1-2) 2002-P uncirculated and proof silver dollars, (3-4) 2002-W uncirculated and proof gold $5	940.00

First Flight Centennial Set	Value
(1) 2003-P proof clad half dollar, (2) 2003-P proof silver dollar, (3) 2003-P proof gold $10	575.00

Lewis and Clark Bicentennial Sets | Value

(1) 2004-P proof silver dollar, (2) Indian pouch — 100.00

(1) 2004-P uncirculated silver dollar, (2) silver-plated bronze Jefferson peace medal replica, (3) 2004-P uncirculated Westward Journey nickel peace-medal design, (4) 2004-P uncirculated Westward Journey nickel keelboat design, (5) 2004-P uncirculated Sacagawea dollar, (6) 1901 $10 U.S. Note replica, (7-9) Lewis and Clark commemorative postage stamps.

125th Anniversary of the Light Bulb Set | Value

(1) 2004-P uncirculated silver dollar, (2) lighted presentation case — 60.00

Marines 1775-2005 Set | Value

(1) 2005-P uncirculated silver dollar, (2) original 1943 Iwo Jima commemorative 3-cent stamp — 75.00

Chief Justice John Marshall Set | Value

(1) 2005-P uncirculated silver dollar, (2) Bureau of Engraving and Printing intaglio print of Marshall — 60.00

2005 American Legacy Set	Value
(1) 2005-P proof Marines 1775-2005 silver dollar, (2) 2005-P proof Chief Justice John Marshall silver dollar, (3) 2005-S proof Lincoln cent, (4) 2005-S proof Westward Journey nickel bison design, (5) 2005-S proof Westward Journey nickel "Ocean in view!" design, (6) 2005-S proof Roosevelt dime, (7) 2005-S proof Minnesota quarter, (8) 2005-S proof Oregon quarter, (9) 2005-S proof Kansas quarter, (10) 2005-S West Virginia proof quarter, (11) 2005-S California proof quarter, (12) 2005-S proof Kennedy half dollar, (13) 2005-S proof Sacagawea dollar	150.00

Benjamin Franklin Tercentenary Set	Value
(1) 2006-P uncirculated silver dollar kite-flying design, (2-5) Franklin commemorative postage stamps, (6) Poor Richard's Almanack reproduction, (7) Bureau of Engraving and Printing intaglio print	65.00

2006 American Legacy Set Set	Value
(1) 2006-P proof Benjamin Franklin Tercentenary portrait design silver dollar, (2) 2006-S proof San Francisco Old Mint silver dollar, (3) 2006-S proof Lincoln cent, (4) 2006-S proof Jefferson nickel, (5) 2006-S proof Roosevelt dime, (6) 2006-S proof Nevada quarter, (7) 2006-S proof Nebraska quarter, (8) 2006-S proof Colorado quarter, (9) 2006-S proof North Dakota quarter, (10) 2006-S proof South Dakota quarter, (11) 2006-S proof Kennedy half dollar, (12) 2006-S proof Sacagawea dollar	150.00

Desegregation in Education Set	Value
(1) 2007-P uncirculated silver dollar, (2) bronze Little Rock Nine official U.S. Mint medal	45.00

2007 American Legacy Set	Value
(1) 2007-P proof Founding of Jamestown 1607-2007 silver dollar, (2) 2007-P proof Desegregation in Education silver dollar, (3) 2007-S proof Lincoln cent, (4) 2007-S proof Jefferson nickel, (5) 2007-S proof Roosevelt dime, (6) 2007-S proof Montana quarter, (7) 2007-S proof Washington state quarter, (8) 2007-S Idaho quarter, (9) 2007-S Wyoming quarter, (10) 2007-S Utah quarter, (11) 2007-S proof Kennedy half dollar, (12) 2007-S proof Sacagawea dollar, (13) 2007-S proof George Washington dollar, (14) 2007-S proof John Adams dollar, (15) 2007-S proof Thomas Jefferson dollar, (16) 2007-S proof James Madison dollar	250.00

Bald Eagle Sets	Value
(1) 2008-S proof half dollar, (2) 2008-P proof silver dollar, (3) 2008-W proof gold $5	400.00
(1) 2008-P uncirculated silver dollar, (2) bald-eagle medal from National Wildlife Refuge System Centennial Medal Series	50.00

2008 American Legacy Set	Value
(1) 2008-P proof Bald Eagle silver dollar, (2) 2008-S proof Lincoln cent, (3) 2008-S proof Jefferson nickel, (4) 2008-S proof Roosevelt dime, (5) 2008-S proof Oklahoma quarter, (6) 2008-S proof New Mexico quarter, (7) 2008-S proof Arizona quarter, (8) 2008-S proof Alaska quarter, (9) 2008-S proof Hawaii quarter, (10) 2008-S proof Kennedy half dollar, (11) 2008-S proof Sacagawea dollar, (12) 2008-S proof James Monroe dollar, (13) 2008-S proof John Quincy Adams dollar, (14) 2008-S proof Andrew Jackson dollar, (15) 2008-S proof Martin Van Buren dollar	200.00

Abraham Lincoln Set	Value
(1) 2009-P proof Abraham Lincoln silver dollar, (2) 2009-S proof Lincoln cent log-cabin design, (3) 2009-S proof Lincoln cent Lincoln-reading design, (4) 2009-S proof Lincoln cent Illinois Old State Capitol design, (5) 2009-S proof Lincoln cent U.S. Capitol design	120.00

Annual mint sets traditionally contain uncirculated examples of the year's circulating coinage.

UNCIRCULATED SETS (1984-)

The U.S. Mint began offering uncirculated sets—also commonly called mint sets—in 1947 as a way for collectors to obtain pristine examples of current-year coinage. They have been offered in most years since; no uncirculated sets were offered in 1982 and 1983.

Uncirculated sets have traditionally contained one example of each coin struck for circulation in their year of issue, including one example of each mintmark for a particular denomination. Coins in uncirculated sets are struck using conventional production methods, but they receive special handling and packaging at the mint.

Coins are sometimes removed from their original Mint packaging on the secondary market and sold individually. These account for the individual uncirculated examples of late-date coins sold at shows and shops, and through advertisements in coin-collecting magazines.

Current-year sets can be purchased directly from the U.S. Mint (www.usmint.gov). Sets from previous years can be purchased on the secondary market at the going price.

In years when the Mint did not offer mint sets, some private companies compiled and marketed uncirculated sets. Values listed below are for officially issued U.S. Mint uncirculated sets in their original packaging.

Date	Sets Sold	Value
1984	1,832,857	3.65
1985	1,710,571	4.40
1986	1,153,536	8.75
1987	2,890,758	5.00
1988	1,646,204	4.50
1989	1,987,915	4.00
1990	1,809,184	4.25
1991	1,352,101	5.50
1992	1,500,143	5.00
1993	1,297,094	5.50
1994	1,234,813	4.40
1995	1,038,787	7.25
1996	1,457,949	15.00
1997	950,473	12.50
1998	1,187,325	4.50
1999	1,421,625	12.75

Date	Sets Sold	Value
2000	1,490,160	10.25
2001	1,066,900	15.85
2002	1,139,388	21.00
2003	1,002,555	16.75
2004	844,484	31.50
2005	–	9.75
2006	–	14.00
2007	–	26.50
2008	–	46.50
2009	–	28.00
2010	–	–

PROOF SETS (1982-)

Proof coins are struck from specially selected, highly polished planchets and dies. They usually receive multiple strikes from the coining press at increased pressure. The results are coins with mirror-like surfaces and, in recent years, a cameo effect on their raised design surfaces.

The coins are then carefully handled; placed in sealed, inert holders; and sold to collectors by the U.S. Mint in sets. Traditionally, the sets contain one proof example of each coin struck for circulation that year, but with the proliferation of commemorative coins and other special issues, such as the 50 State Quarters, the Mint has offered multiple proof sets in a single year.

Prestige Sets, for example, combine proof examples of circulation coinage and half-dollar and dollar commemorative coins from the year of issue. Silver proof sets feature dimes, quarters, and half dollars struck in the traditional 90-percent-silver composition. Silver Premier Sets contain the same coins as the regular silver proof sets but feature special packaging.

The 50 State Quarters and 2009 District of Columbia and U.S. Territories quarters are included in regular proof sets for their respective years but were also offered in separate five-piece sets containing only the quarters.

Proof sets contain only one example of each coin (no multiple mintmarks). Most proof coins are struck at the San Francisco Mint and have an "S" mintmark.

In 1983, some proof sets contain dimes with no "S" mintmark, which was a production error. In 1990, some proof sets contain one-cent coins with no "S" mintmark, also the result of a production error.

Current-year sets can be purchased directly from the U.S. Mint (www.usmint.gov). Sets from previous years can be purchased on the secondary market at the going price. Values listed below are for officially issued U.S. Mint proof sets in their original packaging.

Date	Sets Sold	Value
1982	3,857,479	3.25
1983	3,138,765	5.00
1983 with no-mintmark dime	Inc. above	1,050.00
1983 Prestige Set	140,361	60.00
1984	2,748,430	5.50
1984 Prestige Set	316,680	23.00
1985	3,362,821	4.45
1986	2,411,180	4.95
1986 Prestige Set	599,317	23.00

Date	Sets Sold	Value
1987	3,972,233	3.75
1987 Prestige Set	435,495	20.50
1988	3,031,287	5.00
1988 Prestige Set	231,661	24.50
1989	3,009,107	6.50
1989 Prestige Set	211,087	32.00
1990	2,793,433	5.25
1990 with no-mintmark cent	3,555	5,750.00
1990 Prestige Set	506,126	22.75
1990 Prestige Set with no mintmark-cent	Inc. above	5,800.00
1991	2,610,833	9.65
1991 Prestige Set	256,954	48.50
1992	2,675,618	4.50
1992 Prestige Set	183,285	53.50
1992 silver	1,009,585	13.50
1992 silver Premier Set	308,055	13.50

1992-S Proof Set

Date	Sets Sold	Value
1993	2,337,819	8.85
1993 Prestige Set	224,045	28.00
1993 silver	570,213	23.50
1993 silver Premier Set	191,140	23.50
1994	2,308,701	7.85
1994 Prestige Set	175,893	36.50
1994 silver	636,009	26.50
1994 silver Premier Set	149,320	26.50
1995	2,010,384	21.00
1995 Prestige Set	107,112	110.00
1995 silver	549,878	66.50
1995 silver Premier Set	130,107	66.50

Date	Sets Sold	Value
1996	2,085,191	13.65
1996 Prestige Set	55,000	335.00
1996 silver	623,665	31.50
1996 silver Premier Set	151,366	31.50
1997	1,975,000	21.50
1997 Prestige Set	80,000	110.00
1997 silver	605,473	48.50
1997 silver Premier Set	136,205	48.50
1998	2,078,494	10.75
1998 silver	638,134	18.50
1998 silver Premier Set	240,658	18.50
1999	2,557,899	36.50
1999 5-piece quarters set	1,169,958	34.50
1999 silver	804,565	250.00

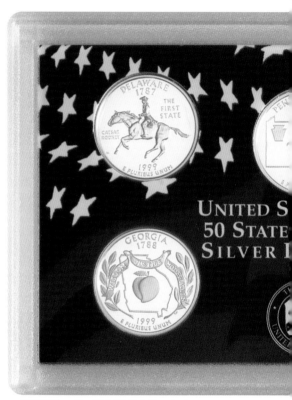

1999-S Silver Proof Set (50 State Quarters)

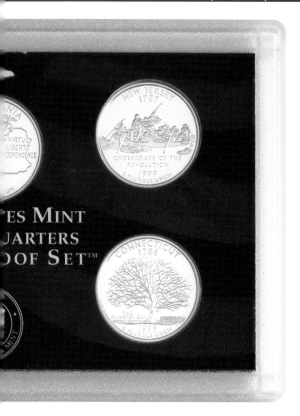

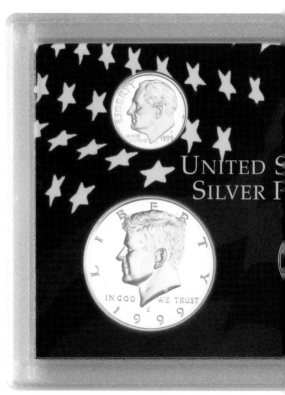

1999-S Silver Proof Set (obverses)

1999-S Silver Proof Set (reverses)

Date	Sets Sold	Value
2000	3,097,442	9.85
2000 5-piece quarters set	995,803	6.00
2000 silver	965,421	27.50

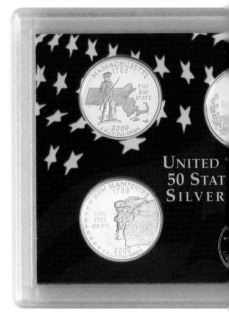

2000-S Silver Proof Set (50 State Quarters)

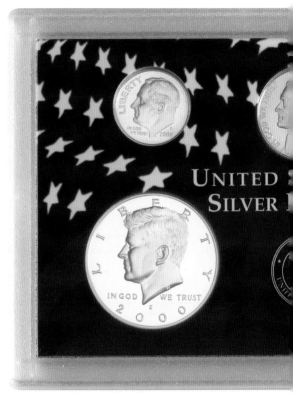

2000-S Silver Proof Set (obverses)

2000-S Silver Proof Set (reverses)

Date	Sets Sold	Value
2001	2,249,498	77.50
2001 5-piece quarters set	774,800	39.50
2001 silver	849,600	105.00

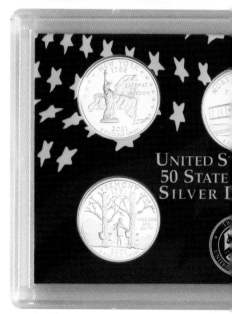

2001-S Silver Proof Set (50 State Quarters)

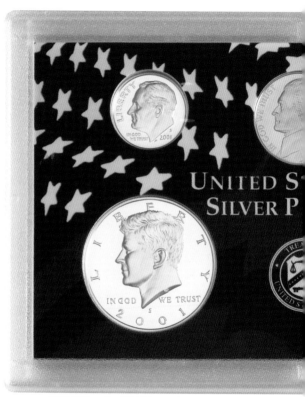

2001-S Silver Proof Set (obverses)

2001-S Silver Proof Set (reverses)

Date	Sets Sold	Value
2002	2,319,766	27.00
2002 5-piece quarters set	764,419	16.50
2002 silver	892,229	66.50

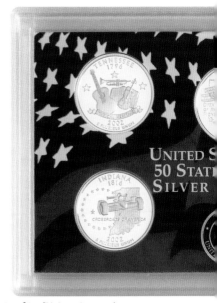

2002-S Silver Proof Set (50 State Quarters)

2002-S Silver Proof Set (obverses)

ATES MINT
ROOF SET™

2002-S Silver Proof Set (reverses)

Date	Sets Sold	Value
2003	2,175,684	16.75
2003 5-piece quarters set	1,225,507	10.00
2003 silver	1,142,858	27.50

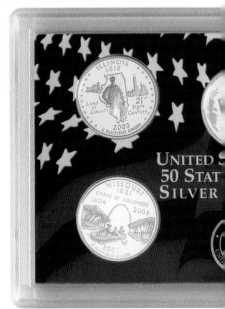

2003-S Silver Proof Set (50 State Quarters)

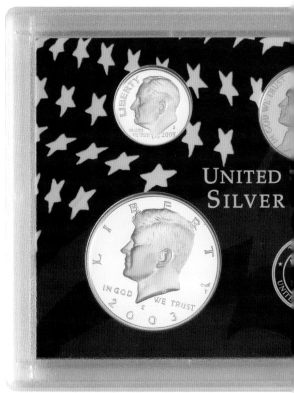

2003-S Silver Proof Set (obverses)

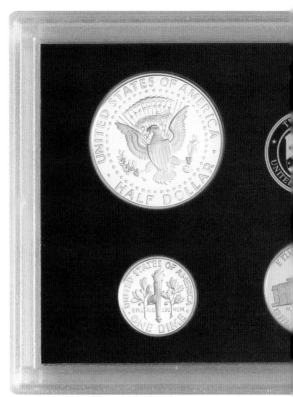

2003-S Silver Proof Set (reverses)

Date	Sets Sold	Value
2004	1,804,396	28.00
2004 5-piece quarters set	987,960	11.00
2004 silver	1,187,673	28.00
2004 silver 5-piece quarters set	594,137	16.00

2004-S Silver Proof Set (50 State Quarters)

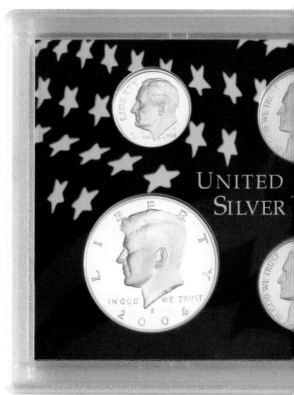

2004-S Silver Proof Set (obverses)

2004-S Silver Proof Set (reverses)

Date	Sets Sold	Value
2005	—	12.50
2005 5-piece quarters set	—	8.85
2005 silver	—	28.50
2005 silver 5-piece quarters set	—	16.00

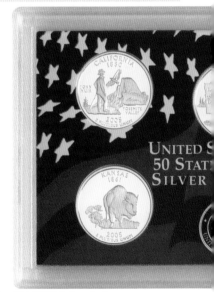

2005 Silver Proof Set (50 State Quarters)

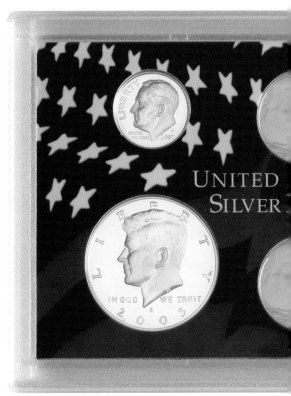

2005-S Silver Proof Set (obverses)

ATES MINT
OOF SET™

2005-S Silver Proof Set (reverses)

Date	Sets Sold	Value
2006	—	28.50
2006 5-piece quarters set	—	14.50
2006 silver	—	30.00
2006 silver 5-piece quarters set	—	17.00

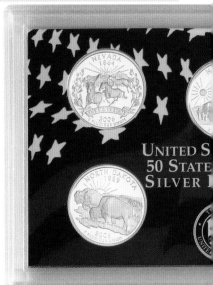

2006-S Silver Proof Set (50 State Quarters)

ES MINT
ARTERS
OF SET™

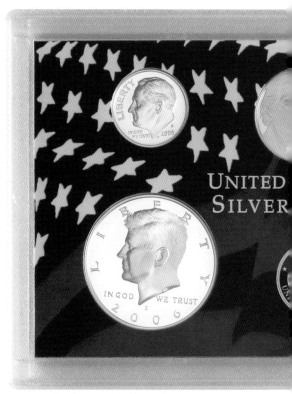

2006-S Silver Proof Set (obverses)

2006-S Silver Proof Set (reverses)

Date	Sets Sold	Value
2007	—	33.50
2007 5-piece quarters set	—	15.25
2007 silver	—	49.50
2007 silver 5-piece quarters set	—	19.00
2007 4-piece Presidential Dollars set	—	20.75

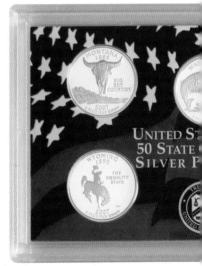

2007-S Silver Proof Set (50 State Quarters)

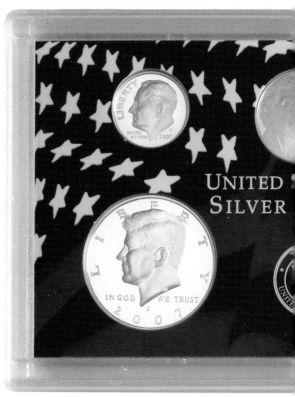

UNITED
SILVER

2007-S Silver Proof Set

2007-S Proof Set (Presidential Dollars)

Date	Sets Sold	Value
2008	—	69.00
2008 5-piece quarters set	—	33.00
2008 4-piece Presidential Dollars set	—	22.00
2008 silver	—	66.50
2008 silver 5-piece quarters set	—	26.50

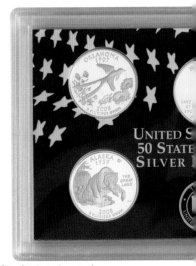

2008-S Silver Proof Set (50 State Quarters)

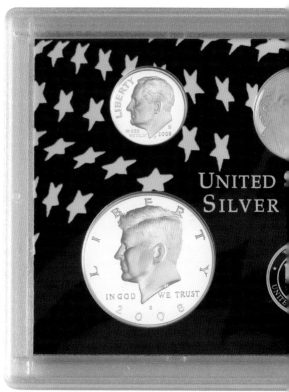

2008-S Silver Proof Set

ATES MINT
ROOF SET™

2008-S Proof Set (Presidential Dollars)

Date	Sets Sold	Value
2009	—	30.00
2009 4-piece Lincoln Bicentennial Cents set	—	10.00
2009 6-piece quarters set	—	15.00
2009 4-piece Presidential Dollar set	—	15.00
2009 silver	—	53.00
2009 6-piece silver quarters set	—	30.00

2009-S Silver Proof Set (D.C. and Territories Quarters)

2009-S Silver Proof Set (obverses)

2009-S Silver Proof Set (reverses)

2009-S Proof Set (Lincoln Bicentennial Cents obverses)

2009-S Proof Set (Lincoln Bicentennial Cents reverses)

2009-S Proof Set (Presidential Dollars)

Date	Sets Sold	Value
2010	—	—
2010 5-piece quarters set	—	15.00
2010 4-piece Presidential Dollars set	—	16.00
2010 silver	—	—
2010 5-piece silver quarters set	—	—

SILVER AMERICAN EAGLE BULLION COINS (1986-)

Silver American Eagle bullion coins are produced and sold as a convenient way for private citizens to invest in precious metals. They contain one ounce of .999-fine silver. They are legal tender and have a nominal face value of $1, but they are not intended to circulate.

The obverse was adapted from Adolph A. Weinman's Walking Liberty design used on the half dollar of 1916-1947. The heraldic eagle on the reverse is a contemporary design by U.S. Mint designer John Mercanti.

Regular strikes of silver American Eagle bullion coins can be purchased from coin and bullion dealers. The Mint does not sell them directly to the public. Instead, the Mint sells bulk quantities to distributors, who in turn wholesale the coins to retailers.

In 1995, the Mint produced a proof silver Eagle with a "W" mintmark (West Point). It was available only in Eagle proof sets celebrating the series' 10th anniversary.

In 2006, to celebrate the silver Eagle's 20th anniversary, the Philadelphia Mint produced a special "reverse proof" in addition to the regular West Point proof version for that year. The reverse proof features a frosted finish in the field and a mirror-like finish on the raised design surfaces, just the opposite (or reverse) of a traditional proof. The 2006 reverse proofs have a "P" mintmark

(Philadelphia) and were available only in a three-coin silver Eagle set (proof, uncirculated, and reverse-proof versions).

From 2006-2008, the Mint sold current-year uncirculated versions struck on specially burnished planchets. The Mint did not offer proof and uncirculated silver Eagles in 2009. Heavy demand for business strikes of silver Eagles forced the Mint to concentrate on regular production of the coins.

Reverse of 2007.

Reverse of 2008.

For 2008, two reverse types appear on the burnished uncirculated silver Eagles, the result of a design modification to the dies. The two types are most easily distinguished by examining the "U" in "United States." On one type—commonly referred to as the "reverse of 2007"—the "U" is bowl shaped. On the other type—commonly referred to as the "reverse of 2008"—the "U" has a spur on its right side. The reverse of 2007 is the more valuable type.

Retail prices for regular strikes in circulated grades are based on the current price of silver bullion plus a small premium.

Diameter: 40.6 millimeters. **Weight:** 31.101 grams. **Composition:** 99.93-percent silver, .07-percent copper. **Actual silver weight:** .999 troy ounces.

Date	Mintage	Unc.	Proof
1986	5,393,005	25.50	—
1986-S	1,446,778	—	50.00
1987	11,442,335	25.00	—
1987-S	904,732	—	50.00

1986-S Proof Silver Eagle $1
Photos courtesy of Heritage Auction Galleries.

Date	Mintage	Unc.	Proof
1988	5,004,646	25.00	—
1988-S	557,370	—	52.00

1988-S Proof Silver Eagle $1 (obverse) Photo courtesy of Heritage Auction Galleries.

1988-S Proof Silver Eagle $1 (reverse) Photo courtesy of Heritage Auction Galleries.

Date	Mintage	Unc.	Proof
1989	5,203,327	22.00	—
1989-S	617,694	—	52.00

1989 Silver Eagle $1 (obverse) Photo courtesy of Heritage Auction Galleries.

1989 Silver Eagle $1 (reverse) Photo courtesy of Heritage Auction Galleries.

Date	Mintage	Unc.	Proof
1990	5,840,210	26.00	—
1990-S	695,510	—	50.00
1991	7,191,066	25.00	—
1991-S	511,924	—	50.00

1990-S Proof Silver Eagle $1 (obverse) Photo courtesy of Heritage Auction Galleries.

1990-S Proof Silver Eagle $1 (reverse) Photo courtesy of Heritage Auction Galleries.

Date	Mintage	Unc.	Proof
1992	5,540,068	25.00	—
1992-S	498,552	—	52.00
1993	6,763,762	25.00	—
1993-P	403,625	—	135.00

1992-S Proof Silver Eagle $1 (obverse) Photo courtesy of Heritage Auction Galleries.

1992-S Proof Silver Eagle $1 (reverse) Photo courtesy of Heritage Auction Galleries.

Date	Mintage	Unc.	Proof
1994	4,227,319	26.00	—
1994-P	372,168	—	215.00

1994-P Proof Silver Eagle $1 (obverse) Photo courtesy of Heritage Auction Galleries.

1994-P Proof Silver Eagle $1 (reverse) Photo courtesy of Heritage Auction Galleries.

Date	Mintage	Unc.	Proof
1995	4,672,051	27.00	—
1995-P	395,400	—	127.00
1995-W	30,125	—	3,150.00
1996	3,603,386	47.00	—
1996-P	473,021	—	85.00
1997	4,295,004	25.00	—
1997-P	429,682	—	132.00
1998	4,847,549	26.00	—
1998-P	452,319	—	45.00
1999	7,408,640	26.00	—
1999-P	549,769	—	47.00
2000	9,239,132	25.00	—
2000-P	600,000	—	50.00
2001	9,001,711	22.00	—
2001-W	746,154	—	50.00

1995-W Proof Silver Eagle $1
Photos courtesy of Heritage Auction Galleries.

Date	Mintage	Unc.	Proof
2002	10,539,026	22.00	—
2002-W	647,342	—	50.00

2002-W Proof Silver Eagle $1 (obverse) Photo courtesy of Heritage Auction Galleries.

2002-W Proof Silver Eagle $1 (reverse) Photo courtesy of Heritage Auction Galleries.

Date	Mintage	Unc.	Proof
2003	8,495,008	22.00	—
2003-W	747,831	—	50.00

2003-W Proof Silver Eagle $1 (obverse) Photo courtesy of Heritage Auction Galleries.

2003-W Proof Silver Eagle $1 (reverse) Photo courtesy of Heritage Auction Galleries.

Date	Mintage	Unc.	Proof
2004	8,882,754	22.00	—
2004-W	783,219	—	50.00
2005	8,891,025	22.00	—
2005-W	823,000	—	50.00

2004-W Proof Silver Eagle $1

Date	Mintage	Unc.	Proof
2006	10,676,522	24.00	—
2006-W burnished	470,000	75.00	—
2006-W	—	—	50.00
2006-P reverse proof	250,000	—	200.00
2006 20th anniversary 3-piece set	—	—	310.00

2006 Proof Silver Eagle $1

Date	Mintage	Unc.	Proof
2007	9,028,036	22.00	—
2007-W burnished	—	20.00	—
2007-W	—	—	50.00

2007-W Proof Silver Eagle $1 (obverse) Photo courtesy of Heritage Auction Galleries.

2007-W Proof Silver Eagle $1 (reverse) Photo courtesy of Heritage Auction Galleries.

Date	Mintage	Unc.	Proof
2008	20,583,000	22.00	—
2008-W burnished	—	23.50	—
2008-W burnished, reverse of 2007	est. 47,000	465.00	—
2008-W	—	—	80.00

2008 Silver Eagle $1

Date	Mintage	Unc.	Proof
2009	30,459,000	22.00	—
2010	—	—	—

2009 Silver Eagle $1
Photos courtesy of Heritage Auction Galleries.

2010 Silver Eagle $1
Photos courtesy of Heritage Auction Galleries.

SILVER AMERICA THE BEAUTIFUL BULLION COINS (2010-2021)

The America's Beautiful National Parks Quarter Dollar Coin Act of 2008 also requires the U.S. Mint to strike silver bullion replicas of the America the Beautiful Quarters.

The bullion versions' designs will be exact duplicates of the circulating quarters, including the denomination "Quarter Dollar." Their diameter, however, will be three inches. They will weigh five ounces and will contain .999-fine silver. The fineness and weight will appear as incused edge lettering on the coins.

Similar to other U.S. bullion coins, the U.S. Mint will sell the coins to authorized purchasers only. These primary purchasers will then sell the coins to the public or other retailers. The authorizing legislation also allows the Mint to sell bulk quantities of the coins to the National Park Service, which in turn can sell the coins to the public.

The Mint can sell an individual America the Beautiful bullion coin to its primary purchasers only in the year in which the corresponding circulating quarter is issued. Thus, the bullion versions will be released in the same year that the corresponding circulating versions are released.

Hot Springs National Park
Location: Arkansas. Established: 1832.

Yellowstone National Park
Location: Wyoming. Established: 1872.

Yosemite National Park
Location: California. Established: 1890.

Grand Canyon National Park
Location: Arizona. Established: 1893.

Mount Hood National Forest
Location: Oregon. Established: 1893.

The bullion versions' designs will be exact duplicates of the circulating America the Beautiful quarters (obverse of circulating quarter seen here). However, their diameter will be three inches and will weigh five ounces and will contain .999-fine silver.

2011 Location	Site	Est.
Pennsylvania	Gettysburg National Military Park	1895
Montana	Glacier National Park	1897
Washington	Olympic National Park	1897
Mississippi	Vicksburg National Military Park	1899
Oklahoma	Chickasaw National Recreation Area	1902

2012 Location	Site	Est.
Puerto Rico	El Yunque National Forest	1903
New Mexico	Chaco Culture National Historical Park	1907
Maine	Acadia National Park	1916
Hawaii	Hawai'i Volcanoes National Park	1916
Alaska	Denali National Park	1917

2013 Location	Site	Est.
New Hampshire	White Mountain National Forest	1918
Ohio	Perry's Victory and International Peace Memorial	1919
Nevada	Great Basin National Park	1922
Maryland	Fort McHenry National Monument and Historic Shrine	1925
South Dakota	Mount Rushmore National Memorial	1925

2014 Location	Site	Est.
Tennessee	Great Smoky Mountains National Park	1926
Virginia	Shenandoah National Park	1926
Utah	Arches National Park	1929
Colorado	Great Sand Dunes National Park	1932
Florida	Everglades National Park	1934

2015 Location	Site	Est.
Nebraska	Homestead National Monument of America	1936
Louisiana	Kisatchie National Forest	1936
North Carolina	Blue Ridge Parkway	1936
Delaware	Bombay Hook National Wildlife Refuge	1937
New York	Saratoga National Historical Park	1938

2016 Location	Site	Est.
Illinois	Shawnee National Forest	1939
Kentucky	Cumberland Gap National Historical Park	1940
West Virginia	Harpers Ferry National Historical Park	1944
North Dakota	Theodore Roosevelt National Park	1946
South Carolina	Fort Moultrie (Fort Sumter National Monument)	1948

2017 Location	Site	Est.
Iowa	Effigy Mounds National Monument	1949
District of Columbia	Frederick Douglass National Historic Site	1962
Missouri	Ozark National Scenic Riverways	1964
New Jersey	Ellis Island National Monument (Statue of Liberty)	1965
Indiana	George Rogers Clark National Historical Park	1966

2018 Location	Site	Est.
Michigan	Pictured Rocks National Lakeshore	1966
Wisconsin	Apostle Islands National Lakeshore	1970
Minnesota	Voyageurs National Park	1971
Georgia	Cumberland Island National Seashore	1972
Rhode Island	Block Island National Wildlife Refuge	1973

2019 Location	Site	Est.
Massachusetts	Lowell National Historical Park	1978
Northern Mariana Islands	American Memorial Park	1978
Guam	War in the Pacific National Historical Park	1978
Texas	San Antonio Missions National Historical Park	1978
Idaho	Frank Church-River of No Return Wilderness	1980

2020 Location	Site	Est.
American Samoa	National Park of American Samoa	1988
Connecticut	Weir Farm National Historic Site	1990
U.S. Virgin Islands	Salt River Bay National Historical Park and Ecological Preserve	1992
Vermont	Marsh-Billings-Rockefeller National Historical Park	1992
Kansas	Tallgrass Prairie National Preserve	1996

2021 Location	Site	Est.
Alabama	Tuskegee Airmen National Historic Site	1998

GOLD AMERICAN EAGLE BULLION COINS (1986-)

Gold American Eagle bullion coins are produced and sold as a convenient way for private citizens to invest in precious metals. They compete in the world gold market with similar issues from other countries, such as South Africa's Krugerrand series and Canada's Maple Leaf series.

Gold American Eagle bullion coins are legal tender and have nominal face values, but they are not intended for circulation. They range in sizes from one-tenth of a troy ounce to one troy ounce and are .9167 fine.

The obverse was adapted from Augustus Saint-Gaudens' design used on the gold $20 coin of 1907-1933, which many consider to be the most beautiful coin in U.S. history. The reverse, which shows a family of eagles with the adult returning to her young in a nest, is a contemporary design by sculptor Miley Busiek. From 1986-1991, the coins were dated with Roman numerals, in the style of Saint-Gaudens' original gold $20.

Regular strikes of gold American Eagle bullion coins can be purchased from coin and precious-metals dealers. The Mint does not sell them directly to the public. Instead, the Mint sells bulk quantities to distributors, who in turn wholesale the coins to retailers.

Proof versions of the one-ounce gold Eagle had been offered since the series' inception in 1986, but proof production of gold Eagles in all sizes was suspended in 2009 because of heavy demand for regular strikes. Proof versions of the half-ounce had been offered since 1987, and proof versions of the tenth-ounce and quarter-ounce had been offered since 1988.

From 2006-2008, the Mint sold current-year uncirculated versions of gold Eagles struck on specially burnished planchets, but production was suspended in 2009 because of heavy demand for regular strikes of the gold Eagles. The burnished uncirculated coins have a "W" mintmark (West Point) and were sold directly to the public by the Mint.

Retail prices for regular strikes in circulated grades are based on the current price of gold bullion plus a small premium.

In 1999, the West Point Mint mistakenly struck tenth-ounce and quarter-ounce gold Eagles with proof dies that did not receive the special polishing customary of proof dies. The result was uncirculated-quality coins with a "W" mintmark. Only the proof versions should have had the "W" mintmark.

In 2006, to celebrate the gold Eagle's 20th anniversary, the West Point Mint produced a special "reverse proof" of the one-ounce gold Eagle in addition to the regular West Point proof version for that year. The reverse proof features a frosted finish in the field and a mirrorlike finish on the raised design surfaces, just the opposite (or reverse) of a traditional proof. The 2006 reverse proofs have a "W" mintmark and were available only in a three-coin one-ounce gold Eagle set (proof, reverse proof, and uncirculated).

Composition: 91.67-percent gold (22 karats), 5.33-percent copper, 3-percent silver.

Tenth Ounce ($5)

Diameter: 16.5 millimeters. **Weight:** 3.393 grams. **Actual gold weight:** .100 troy ounces.

Date	Mintage	Unc.	Proof
MCMLXXXVI (1986)	912,609	160.00	—
MCMLXXXVII (1987)	580,266	150.00	—
MCMLXXXVIII (1988)	159,500	200.00	—
MCMLXXXVIII-P (1988)	143,881	—	230.00

1993-P Proof Gold American Eagle $5
Photos courtesy of Heritage Auction Galleries.

Date	Mintage	Unc.	Proof
MCMLXXXIX (1989)	264,790	150.00	—
MCMLXXXIX-P (1989)	82,924	—	235.00
MCMXC (1990)	210,210	150.00	—
MCMXC-P (1990)	99,349	—	235.00
MCMXCI (1991)	165,200	160.00	—
MCMXCI-P (1991)	70,344	—	230.00
1992	209,300	150.00	—
1992-P	64,902	—	230.00
1993	210,709	150.00	—
1993-P	58,649	—	230.00
1994	206,380	150.00	—
1994-W	62,100	—	230.00
1995	223,025	150.00	—
1995-W	62,650	—	230.00
1996	401,964	150.00	—
1996-W	58,440	—	230.00
1997	528,515	150.00	—
1997-W	35,000	—	230.00

Date	Mintage	Unc.	Proof
1998	1,344,520	150.00	—
1998-W	39,653	—	230.00

1998 Gold American Eagle $5
Photos courtesy of Heritage Auction Galleries.

Date	Mintage	Unc.	Proof
1999	2,750,338	150.00	—
1999-W	48,426	—	165.00
1999-W die error	—	575.00	—

1999-W Proof Gold American Eagle $5 (Struck with unfinished proof die.)
Photos courtesy of Heritage Auction Galleries.

Date	Mintage	Unc.	Proof
2000	569,153	225.00	—
2000-W	50,000	—	230.00

2000 Gold American Eagle $5
Photos courtesy of Heritage Auction Galleries.

Date	Mintage	Unc.	Proof
2001	260,147	150.00	—
2001-W	37,547	—	230.00
2002	230,027	150.00	—
2002-W	40,864	—	230.00
2003	245,029	150.00	—
2003-W	40,634	—	230.00
2004	250,016	150.00	—
2004-W	35,481	—	230.00

2002 Gold American Eagle $5
Photos courtesy of Heritage Auction Galleries.

Date	Mintage	Unc.	Proof
2005	300,043	150.00	—
2005-W	48,455	—	230.00
2006	237,510	150.00	—
2006-W burnished	—	150.00	—
2006-W	—	—	230.00
2007	190,010	150.00	—
2007-W burnished	—	150.00	—
2007-W	—	—	245.00

2006-W Gold American Eagle $5
Photos courtesy of Heritage Auction Galleries.

2007-W Gold American Eagle $5
Photos courtesy of Heritage Auction Galleries.

Date	Mintage	Unc.	Proof
2008	—	160.00	—
2008-W burnished	—	150.00	—
2008-W	—	—	245.00
2009	270,000	150.00	—
2010	—	—	—

2008-W Gold American Eagle $5
Photos courtesy of Heritage Auction Galleries.

Quarter Ounce ($10)

Diameter: 22 millimeters. **Weight:** 8.483 grams. **Actual gold weight:** .250 troy ounces.

Date	Mintage	Unc.	Proof
MCMLXXXVI (1986)	726,031	340.00	—
MCMLXXXVII (1987)	269,255	335.00	—
MCMLXXXVIII (1988)	49,000	340.00	—
MCMLXXXVIII-P (1988)	98,028	—	450.00

1988 Gold American Eagle $10

Date	Mintage	Unc.	Proof
MCMLXXXIX (1989)	81,789	340.00	—
MCMLXXXIX-P (1989)	53,593	—	450.00
MCMXC (1990)	41,000	340.00	—
MCMXC-P (1990)	62,674	—	450.00
MCMXCI (1991)	36,100	375.00	—
MCMXCI-P (1991)	50,839	—	450.00
1992	59,546	340.00	—
1992-P	46,290	—	450.00
1993	71,864	340.00	—
1993-P	46,271	—	450.00
1994	72,650	340.00	—
1994-W	47,600	—	450.00
1995	83,752	340.00	—
1995-W	47,545	—	450.00
1996	60,318	340.00	—
1996-W	39,190	—	450.00
1997	108,805	340.00	—
1997-W	29,800		450.00

Date	Mintage	Unc.	Proof
1998	309,829	340.00	—
1998-W	29,733	—	450.00
1999	564,232	340.00	—
1999-W	34,416	—	450.00
1999-W die error	—	1,050.00	—

1999-W Proof Gold American Eagle $10 (Struck with unfinished proof die.)
Photos courtesy of Heritage Auction Galleries.

Date	Mintage	Unc.	Proof
2000	128,964	340.00	—
2000-W	36,000	—	450.00
2001	71,280	340.00	—
2001-W	25,630	—	450.00
2002	62,027	340.00	—
2002-W	29,242	—	450.00
2003	74,029	340.00	—
2003-W	31,000	—	450.00

2000-W Gold American Eagle $10
Photos courtesy of Heritage Auction Galleries.

Date	Mintage	Unc.	Proof
2004	72,014	340.00	—
2004-W	29,127	—	450.00

2004 Gold American Eagle $10
Photos courtesy of Heritage Auction Galleries.

Date	Mintage	Unc.	Proof
2005	72,015	340.00	—
2005-W	34,637	—	450.00

2005 Gold American Eagle $10
Photos courtesy of Heritage Auction Galleries.

Date	Mintage	Unc.	Proof
2006	60,004	340.00	—
2006-W burnished	—	335.00	—
2006-W	—	—	450.00
2007	34,004	340.00	—
2007-W burnished	—	420.00	—
2007-W	—	—	555.00
2008	—	340.00	—
2008-W burnished	—	550.00	—
2008-W	—	—	555.00
2009	110,000	340.00	—
2010	—	—	—

2006-W Gold American Eagle $10
Photos courtesy of Heritage Auction Galleries.

Half Ounce ($25)

Diameter: 27 millimeters. **Weight:** 16.966 grams. **Actual gold weight:** .500 troy ounces.

Date	Mintage	Unc.	Proof
MCMLXXXVI (1986)	599,566	660.00	—
MCMLXXXVII (1987)	131,255	635.00	—
MCMLXXXVII-P (1987)	143,398	—	1,100.00
MCMLXXXVIII (1988)	45,000	745.00	—
MCMLXXXVIII-P (1988)	76,528	—	1,100.00

1988 Gold American Eagle $25

Date	Mintage	Unc.	Proof
MCMLXXXIX (1989)	44,829	800.00	—
MCMLXXXIX-P (1989)	44,264	—	1,100.00
MCMXC (1990)	31,000	965.00	—
MCMXC-P (1990)	51,636	—	1,100.00
MCMXCI (1991)	24,100	1,575.00	—
MCMXCI-P (1991)	53,125	—	1,100.00
1992	54,404	655.00	—
1992-P	40,982	—	1,100.00
1993	73,324	655.00	—
1993-P	43,319	—	1,100.00
1994	62,400	655.00	—
1994-W	44,100	—	1,100.00
1995	53,474	645.00	—
1995-W	45,511	—	1,100.00
1996	39,287	655.00	—
1996-W	35,937	—	1,100.00
1997	79,605	655.00	—
1997-W	26,350	—	1,100.00
1998	169,029	655.00	—
1998-W	25,896	—	1,100.00

Date	Mintage	Unc.	Proof
1999	263,013	655.00	—
1999-W	30,452	—	1,100.00
2000	79,287	655.00	—
2000-W	32,000	—	1,100.00
2001	48,047	655.00	—
2001-W	23,261	—	1,100.00
2002	70,027	655.00	—
2002-W	26,646	—	1,100.00

2003 Gold American Eagle $25
Photos courtesy of Heritage Auction Galleries.

Date	Mintage	Unc.	Proof
2003	79,029	655.00	—
2003-W	29,000	—	1,100.00
2004	98,040	655.00	—
2004-W	27,731	—	1,100.00
2005	80,023	655.00	—
2005-W	33,598	—	1,100.00
2006	66,005	660.00	—
2006-W burnished	—	900.00	—
2006-W	—	—	1,100.00
2007	47,002	660.00	—
2007-W burnished	—	845.00	—
2007-W	—	—	1,100.00
2008	—	660.00	—
2008-W burnished	—	660.00	—
2008-W	—	—	1,100.00
2009	110,000	660.00	—
2010	—	—	—

One Ounce ($50)

Diameter: 32.7 millimeters. **Weight:** 33.931 grams. **Actual gold weight:** 1 troy ounce.

Date	Mintage	Unc.	Proof
MCMLXXXVI (1986)	1,362,650	1,250.00	—
MCMLXXXVI-P (1986)	446,290	—	2,135.00

1986 American Gold Eagle $50

1988 Gold American Eagle $50
Photos courtesy of Heritage Auction Galleries.

Date	Mintage	Unc.	Proof
MCMLXXXVII (1987)	1,045,500	1,250.00	—
MCMLXXXVII-W (1987)	147,498	—	2,135.00
MCMLXXXVIII (1988)	465,000	1,250.00	—
MCMLXXXVIII-W (1988)	87,133	—	2,135.00
MCMLXXXIX (1989)	—	1,250.00	—
MCMLXXXIX-W (1989)	53,960	—	2,135.00
MCMXC (1990)	373,210	1,250.00	—
MCMXC-W (1990)	62,401	—	2,135.00
MCMXCI (1991)	243,100	1,250.00	—
MCMXCI-W (1991)	50,411	—	2,135.00
1992	275,000	1,250.00	—
1992-W	44,835	—	2,135.00
1993	480,192	1,250.00	—
1993-W	34,389	—	2,135.00
1994	221,633	1,250.00	—
1994-W	36,300	—	2,135.00

1994-W Proof Gold American Eagle $50
Photos courtesy of Heritage Auction Galleries.

Date	Mintage	Unc.	Proof
1995	200,636	1,250.00	—
1995-W	46,553	—	2,135.00
1996	189,148	1,250.00	—
1996-W	37,302	—	2,135.00
1997	664,508	1,250.00	—
1997-W	28,000	—	2,135.00
1998	1,468,530	1,250.00	—
1998-W	26,060	—	2,145.00
1999	1,505,026	1,250.00	—
1999-W	31,446	—	2,135.00
2000	433,319	1,250.00	—
2000-W	33,000	—	2,135.00
2001	143,605	1,250.00	—
2001-W	24,580	—	2,135.00
2002	222,029	1,250.00	—
2002-W	24,242	—	2,135.00
2003	416,032	1,250.00	—
2003-W	29,000	—	2,135.00
2004	417,019	1,250.00	—
2004-W	28,731	—	2,135.00

2000 Gold American Eagle $50
Photos courtesy of Heritage Auction Galleries.

Date	Mintage	Unc.	Proof
2005	356,555	1,250.00	—
2005-W	34,695	—	2,135.00
2006	237,510	1,250.00	—
2006-W burnished	—	1,125.00	—
2006-W	—	—	2,135.00
2006-W reverse proof	10,000	—	2,200.00
2007	140,016	1,260.00	—
2007-W burnished	—	1,125.00	—
2007-W	—	—	2,135.00
2008	—	1,250.00	—
2008-W burnished	—	1,165.00	—
2008-W	1,493,000	—	2,135.00
2009	—	1,250.00	—
2010	—	1,250.00	—

2006 American Gold Eagle $50

2008-W Gold American Eagle $50
Photos courtesy of Heritage Auction Galleries.

GOLD AMERICAN BUFFALO BULLION COINS (2006-)

Authorization of one-ounce gold bullion coins resurrecting the old Buffalo-nickel design was part of the Presidential $1 Coin Act of 2005. The U.S. Mint billed them as the first "pure" gold coins (24 karats, .9999 fine) in U.S. history when production commenced on June 20, 2006. In 2008, the Mint introduced fractional sizes in the series.

James Earle Fraser's classic and popular design was used on the 5-cent coin from 1913-1938. It features a Native American man on the obverse and a North American bison, commonly called a buffalo, on the reverse.

Fraser's original design showed the buffalo standing on a mound on the reverse, but later in 1913, the design was changed to show the buffalo standing on a line. The American Buffalo bullion coins use the original, mound-type design. Below the buffalo is the coin's nominal denomination and the inscription "1 oz. .9999 Fine Gold."

Bullion coins are produced and sold as a convenient way for the general public to own precious metals. They are not intended for circulation. Values fluctuate with the current price of the precious metal contained in the coin.

The Mint sells business strikes of the American Buffalo bullion coin to authorized purchasers only. These primary purchasers then sell the coins to the public or other retailers. The Mint does sell proof versions of the American Buffalo bullion coin directly to the public.

Tenth-Ounce ($5)

Diameter: 16 millimeters. **Weight:** 3.11 grams. **Composition:** 99.99-percent gold. **Actual gold weight:** .100 troy ounces.

Date	Mintage	Unc.	Proof
2008-W	—	560.00	—
2008-W	—	—	650.00

2008-W Gold American Buffalo $5
Photos courtesy of Heritage Auction Galleries.

Quarter-Ounce ($10)

Diameter: 21.5 millimeters. **Weight:** 7.78 grams. **Composition:** 99.99-percent gold. **Actual gold weight:** .250 troy ounces.

Date	Mintage	Unc.	Proof
2008-W	—	950.00	—
2008-W	—	—	990.00

2008-W Gold American Buffalo $10.
Photos courtesy of Heritage Auction Galleries.

Half-Ounce ($25)

Diameter: 26 millimeters. **Weight:** 16.96 grams. **Composition:** 99.99-percent gold. **Actual gold weight:** .499 troy ounces.

Date	Mintage	Unc.	Proof
2008-W	—	1,285.00	—
2008-W	—	—	1,350.00

2008 Gold American Buffalo $25
Photos courtesy of Heritage Auction Galleries.

One-Ounce ($50)

Diameter: 32.7 millimeters. **Weight:** 31.1 grams. **Composition:** 99.99-percent gold. **Actual gold weight:** 1 troy ounce.

Date	Mintage	Unc.	Proof
2006	337,012	1,300.00	—
2006-W	—	—	1,480.00
2007	136,503	1,300.00	—
2007-W	—	—	1,480.00
2008	—	1,300.00	—
2008-W	—	—	2,385.00
2009	—	1,300.00	—
2009-W	—	—	2,350.00
2010	—	—	—
2010-W	—	—	—

2006 Gold American Buffalo $50
Photos courtesy of Heritage Auction Galleries.

2007-W Proof Gold American Buffalo $50

2008-W Proof Gold American Buffalo $50

2009-W Proof Gold American Buffalo $50
Photos courtesy of Heritage Auction Galleries.

PLATINUM AMERICAN EAGLE BULLION COINS (1997-)

Like their silver and gold counterparts, platinum American Eagle bullion coins are produced and sold as a convenient way for private citizens to invest in precious metals. They are legal tender and have nominal face values, but they are not intended for circulation. They range in sizes from one-tenth of a troy ounce to one troy ounce and are .99995 fine.

Regular strikes of platinum American Eagle bullion coins can be purchased from coin and bullion dealers. The Mint does not sell them directly to the public. Instead, the Mint sells bulk quantities to distributors, who in turn wholesale the coins to retailers.

The common obverse on all platinum Eagle bullion coins is a depiction of the Statue of Liberty by Mint sculptor-engraver John Mercanti. The reverse on regular strikes depicts a soaring eagle by Mint sculptor-engraver Thomas D. Rogers.

Proof versions have been offered since the series' inception in 1997, and current-year proofs can be purchased directly from the U.S. Mint (www.usmint.gov). In 1998, the Mint began offering proof platinum Eagles with a different reverse design each year, paired with the common Statue of Liberty obverse. From 1998-2002, the design theme was Vistas of Liberty and featured national landscapes.

In 2006, a three-year series titled Foundations of American Democracy was introduced. It honored the three branches of U.S. government: legislative, executive, and judicial—in the order in which they are mentioned in the Constitution.

In 2009, a six-year series highlighting the preamble to the Constitution began. In that year, however, the Mint suspended production of all platinum American Eagle bullion coins (regular, uncirculated, and proof strikes in all sizes) except for the proof one-ounce version.

From 2006-2008, the Mint offered current-year uncirculated versions struck on specially burnished planchets. These uncirculated coins were available directly from the Mint. Retail prices for regular strikes in circulated grades are based on the current price of platinum bullion plus a small premium.

Composition: 99.95-percent platinum.

Tenth Ounce ($10)

Diameter: 17 millimeters. **Weight:** 3.110 grams. **Actual platinum weight:** .100 troy ounces.

Date	Mintage	Unc.	Proof
1997	70,250	180.00	–
1997-W	36,996	–	215.00

1997-W Proof Tenth-Ounce Platinum Eagle $10

Date	Mintage	Unc.	Proof
1998	39,525	180.00	–
1998-W	19,832	–	215.00

1998-W Proof Tenth-Ounce Platinum Eagle $10

Date	Mintage	Unc.	Proof
1999	55,955	180.00	–
1999-W	19,123	–	215.00

1999-W Proof Tenth-Ounce Platinum Eagle $10

Date	Mintage	Unc.	Proof
2000	34,027	180.00	–
2000-W	15,651	–	215.00

2000-W Proof Tenth-Ounce Platinum Eagle $10

Date	Mintage	Unc.	Proof
2001	52,017	180.00	–
2001-W	12,193	–	215.00

2001-W Proof Tenth-Ounce Platinum Eagle $10

Date	Mintage	Unc.	Proof
2002	23,005	180.00	–
2002-W	12,365	–	214.00

2002-W Proof Tenth-Ounce Platinum Eagle $10

Date	Mintage	Unc.	Proof
2003	22,007	180.00	–
2003-W	8,161	–	265.00

2003-W Proof Tenth-Ounce Platinum Eagle $10

Date	Mintage	Unc.	Proof
2004	15,010	180.00	–
2004-W	6,846	–	615.00

2004 Tenth-Ounce Platinum Eagle $10
Photos courtesy of Heritage Auction Galleries.

Date	Mintage	Unc.	Proof
2005	14,013	180.00	–
2005-W	8,000	–	235.00

2005 Tenth-Ounce Platinum Eagle $10
Photos courtesy of Heritage Auction Galleries.

Date	Mintage	Unc.	Proof
2006	11,001	180.00	–
2006-W burnished	–	390.00	–
2006-W	–	–	215.00

2006 Tenth-Ounce Platinum Eagle $10
Photos courtesy of Heritage Auction Galleries.

Date	Mintage	Unc.	Proof
2007	13,003	280.00	–
2007-W burnished	–	185.00	–
2007-W	–	–	215.00
2008	–	180.00	–
2008-W burnished	–	190.00	–
2008-W	–	–	410.00

2007-W Tenth-Ounce Platinum Eagle $10
Photos courtesy of Heritage Auction Galleries.

Quarter Ounce ($25)

Diameter: 22 millimeters. **Weight:** 7.785 grams. **Actual platinum weight:** .250 troy ounces.

Date	Mintage	Unc.	Proof
1997	27,100	435.00	–
1997-W	18,628	–	480.00

1997-W Proof Quarter-Ounce Platinum Eagle $25

Date	Mintage	Unc.	Proof
1998	38,887	435.00	–
1998-W	14,860	–	480.00

1998-W Proof Quarter-Ounce Platinum Eagle $25

Date	Mintage	Unc.	Proof
1999	39,734	435.00	–
1999-W	13,514	–	480.00

1999-W Proof Quarter-Ounce Platinum Eagle $25

Date	Mintage	Unc.	Proof
2000	20,054	435.00	–
2000-W	11,995	–	480.00

2000-W Proof Quarter-Ounce Platinum Eagle $25

Date	Mintage	Unc.	Proof
2001	21,815	435.00	–
2001-W	8,858	–	480.00

2001-W Proof Quarter-Ounce Platinum Eagle $25

Date	Mintage	Unc.	Proof
2002	27,405	435.00	–
2002-W	9,282	–	480.00

2002-W Proof Quarter-Ounce Platinum Eagle $25

Date	Mintage	Unc.	Proof
2003	25,207	435.00	–
2003-W	6,045	–	480.00

2003-W Proof Quarter-Ounce Platinum Eagle $25

Date	Mintage	Unc.	Proof
2004	18,010	435.00	–
2004-W	5,035	–	1,190.00

2004-W Proof Quarter-Ounce Platinum Eagle $25

Date	Mintage	Unc.	Proof
2005	12,013	435.00	–
2005-W	6,424	–	530.00
2006	12,001	435.00	–
2006-W burnished	–	585.00	–
2006-W	–	–	445.00
2007	8,402	435.00	–
2007-W burnished	–	450.00	–
2007-W	–	–	500.00
2008	–	435.00	–
2008-W burnished	–	445.00	–
2008-W	–	–	775.00

2006-W Proof Quarter-Ounce Platinum Eagle $25

Half Ounce ($50)

Diameter: 27 millimeters. **Weight:** 15.552 grams. **Actual platinum weight:** .499 troy ounces.

Date	Mintage	Unc.	Proof
1997	20,500	870.00	–
1997-W	15,432	–	1,000.00

1997-W Proof Half-Ounce Platinum Eagle $50

Date	Mintage	Unc.	Proof
1998	32,415	870.00	–
1998-W	13,821	–	1,000.00

1998-W Proof Half-Ounce Platinum Eagle $50

Date	Mintage	Unc.	Proof
1999	32,309	870.00	–
1999-W	11,098	–	1,000.00

1999-W Proof Half-Ounce Platinum Eagle $50

Date	Mintage	Unc.	Proof
2000	18,892	870.00	–
2000-W	11,049	–	1,000.00
2001	12,815	870.00	–
2001-W	8,268	–	1,000.00

2000-W Proof Half-Ounce Platinum Eagle $50

Date	Mintage	Unc.	Proof
2002	24,005	870.00	–
2002-W	8,772	–	1,000.00
2003	17,409	870.00	–
2003-W	6,181	–	1,000.00

2002-W Proof Half-Ounce Platinum Eagle $50

Date	Mintage	Unc.	Proof
2004	–	870.00	–
2004-W	4,886	–	1,775.00

2004-W Proof Half-Ounce Platinum Eagle $50

Date	Mintage	Unc.	Proof
2005	9,013	870.00	–
2005-W	5,720	–	1,025.00

2005-W Proof Half-Ounce Platinum Eagle $50

Date	Mintage	Unc.	Proof
2006	9,602	870.00	–
2006-W burnished	–	885.00	–
2006-W	–	–	1,000.00

2006-W Proof Half-Ounce Platinum Eagle $50

2007-W Proof Half-Ounce Platinum Eagle $50 (10th anniversary proof)
Photos courtesy of Heritage Auction Galleries.

Date	Mintage	Unc.	Proof
2007	–	870.00	–
2007-W burnished	–	980.00	–
2007-W	–	–	1,000.00
2008	–	870.00	–
2008-W burnished	–	885.00	–
2008-W	–	–	1,185.00

2008-W Proof Half-Ounce Platinum Eagle $50
Photos courtesy of Heritage Auction Galleries.

One Ounce ($100)

Diameter: 33 millimeters. **Weight:** 31.105 grams. **Actual platinum weight:** .999 troy ounces.

Date	Mintage	Unc.	Proof
1997	56,000	1,680.00	–
1997-W	15,885	–	1,925.00

1997-W Proof One-Ounce Platinum Eagle $100

Date	Mintage	Unc.	Proof
1998	133,002	1,680.00	–
1998-W	14,203	–	1,910.00

1998-W Proof One-Ounce Platinum Eagle $100

Date	Mintage	Unc.	Proof
1999	56,707	1,680.00	–
1999-W	–	–	1,910.00

1999-W Proof One-Ounce Platinum Eagle $100

Date	Mintage	Unc.	Proof
2000	18,892	1,680.00	–
2000-W	–	–	1,910.00

2000-W Proof One-Ounce Platinum Eagle $100

Date	Mintage	Unc.	Proof
2001	14,070	1,680.00	–
2001-W	8,990	–	1,910.00

2001-W Proof One-Ounce Platinum Eagle $100

Date	Mintage	Unc.	Proof
2002	11,502	1,680.00	–
2002-W	9,834	–	1,910.00

2002-W Proof One-Ounce Platinum Eagle $100

Date	Mintage	Unc.	Proof
2003	8,007	1,680.00	–
2003-W	6,991	–	1,925.00

2003-W Proof One-Ounce platinum Eagle $100

Date	Mintage	Unc.	Proof
2004	7,009	1,680.00	–
2004-W	5,833	–	2,350.00

2004-W Proof One-Ounce Platinum Eagle $100

Date	Mintage	Unc.	Proof
2005	6,310	1,680.00	–
2005-W	6,700	–	1,925.00

2005-W Proof One-Ounce Platinum Eagle $100

Date	Mintage	Unc.	Proof
2006	6,000	1,680.00	–
2006-W burnished	–	1,585.00	–
2006-W	–	–	1,910.00

2006-W Proof One-Ounce Platinum Eagle $100

Date	Mintage	Unc.	Proof
2007	–	1,680.00	–
2007-W burnished	–	1,585.00	–
2007-W	–	–	1,910.00
2008	–	1,680.00	–
2008-W burnished	–	1,690.00	–
2008-W	–	–	2,400.00
2009-W	8,000	–	2,100.00

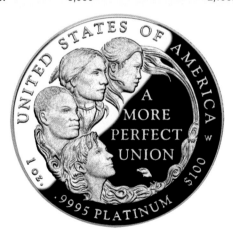

2009-W Proof One-Ounce Platinum Eagle $100 (reverse)

GLOSSARY

Alloy: A metal or mixture of metals added to the primary metal in the coinage composition, often as a means of facilitating hardness during striking. For example, most U.S. silver and gold coins contain an alloy of 90-percent precious metal and 10-percent copper.

Authentication: The act of determining whether a coin, medal, token, or other related item is a genuine product of the issuing authority.

Bag Marks: Scrapes and impairments to a coin's surface obtained after minting by contact with other coins. The term originates from the storage of coins in bags.

Commemorative: An official, government-issued coin to honor a special event or person. Commemoratives are usually sold directly to collectors at a premium above face value by the issuing authority, such as the U.S. Mint.

Counterfeit: A coin, medal, or other numismatic item made fraudulently either for entry into circulation or sale to collectors. In numismatics, counterfeiting can involve outright attempts to produce a rare coin from scratch. It can also involve altering a common coin to make it look like a scarce variety. For instance, a counterfeiter may try to remove the mintmark from a 1982 Roosevelt dime to try to pass it off as one of the scarce 1982 no-mintmark dimes.

Die: A cylindrical piece of metal containing an incuse image of a coin design that imparts a raised image when stamped into a planchet on a coining press.

Edge: The cylindrical surface of a coin between the two sides. The edge can be plain, reeded, ornamented, or lettered.

Face Value: The nominal, legal-tender value assigned to a given coin by the governing authority.

Grading: The largely subjective practice of providing a numerical or adjectival ranking of a coin's condition.

Hub: A piece of die steel showing the coinage devices in relief, or raised, as they are on a coin. The hub is pressed into the blank die, resulting in an incused, mirror image on the die. The die is then pressed into a planchet, or coin blank, on a coining press, to produce a coin.

Lettered Edge: Incused or raised lettering on a coin's edge.

Mintage: The total number of coins struck during a given time frame, generally one year. Coin listings in value guides, such as *Coin Prices* magazine, usually include mintages.

Mintmark: A letter or other marking on a coin's surface to identify the mint at which the coin was struck. Mintmarks currently used on U.S. coins are a "P" for the Philadelphia Mint, "D" for Denver, "S" for San Francisco, and "W" for West Point.

Numismatics, Numismatist:

Numismatics (pronounced "new-miss-MAT-iks") is the science, study, or collecting of coins, tokens, medals, paper money, and related items. One who participates in this science is a numismatist (pronounced "new-MISS-mat-ist").

Planchet: A blank disc of metal on which the image of the dies are impressed in a coining press, resulting in a finished coin. Also sometimes called a "blank."

Proof: A type of coin produced specially for sale to collectors. It is produced from specially polished dies and planchets, and receives more than one striking in the coining press. Modern silver proofs often have what are called "frosted" surfaces, which is a white finish on the raised design devices, such as a bust on the obverse.

Reeding: The serrated (tooth-like) ornamentation applied to a coin's edge during striking. U.S. dimes, quarters, and half dollars currently produced for circulation have reeded edges. The one-cent and five-cent coins have plain edges.

Series: The complete group of coins of the same denomination and design, and representing all issuing mints. For example, the Roosevelt dime series has been struck since 1946. The 50 State Quarters program is another example of a coin series.

Slabs: A nickname for coins graded by a professional coin-grading service and then sealed in a plastic holder with the coin's description, the grade assigned by the service, and a unique serial number.

Type Coin: A coin that is collected because it represents a basic design of a particular denomination. For example, a type set of 20th-century U.S. quarters would consist of one example each of the Barber type (1892-1916), the Standing Liberty type (1916-1930), and the Washington type (1932 to present). Many collectors turn to type collecting because it is easier and provides more financial flexibility than trying to assemble an example of each date and mintmark combination of an entire series. In the quarter type-set example above, type collectors can choose any date and mintmark combination from any of the dates listed for each type. The collecting goal is an example of each design type rather than specific date and mintmark combinations.

Variety: Any coin with a design feature different from the usual design for a particular coin series. The 1982 no-mintmark dime, for example, is a variety of the Roosevelt dime. The "extra-leaf" Wisconsin quarters are varieties of that series.

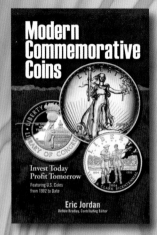

Make the Most of the Modern Commemorative Market

You're sure to have seen commemoratives at shows, club meetings and your local coin shop, but how much do you know about this popular area of collecting? Do you know about the various options for expanding your retirement portfolio with commemoratives? How about which coins ranked the highest among all commemoratives in the last few years?

You'll find the answers to these questions, and much more in this handy and helpful book. Packed with 700+ fantastic color photographs of coins, this book is easy-to-carry and simple to use to identify your modern commemoratives (issued since 1982), and you also will find up-to-date values and advice for where to invest when it comes to commemoratives.

Item#Z7651 • $16.09